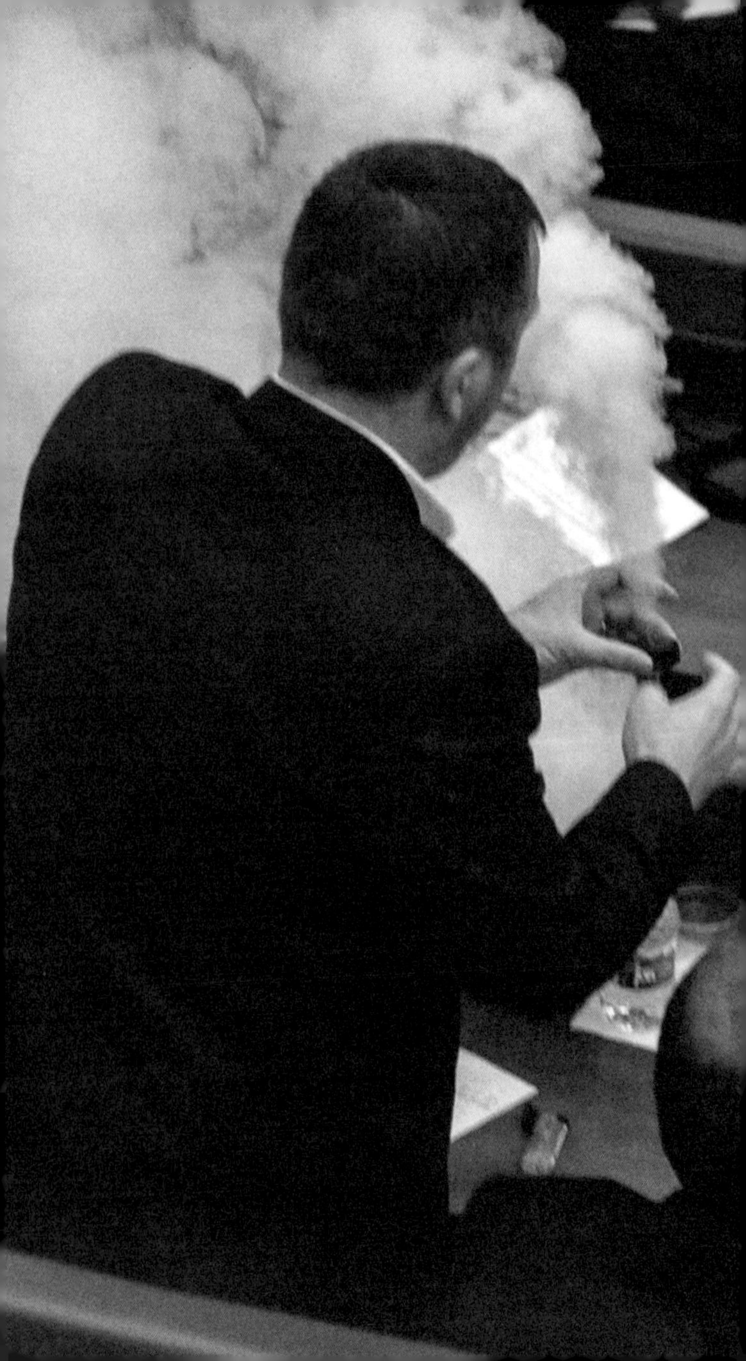

CONTENTS

INTRODUCTION

This publication collects writings on the art scene of Kosovo over the past 20 years.

In the 1990s Kosovars felt—as many other countries in the Balkan region did—the urgency to shape their own scene: in a search for identity, for nation building, in continuing or ending political conflicts, by trying to find a language to grasp recent social and political developments, or simply by continuing their practice in new, unstable times. This collection of writings and interviews tries to offer insights into these processes.

Vesa Sahatçiu gives an overview of the art scene since the late 1990s and looks back at earlier important influences. Shkelzen Maliqi explores the cultural influences, key players, and art institutions from the millennium to the most recent tendencies in his text and in his interview with Edi Muka—arguably the most influential Albanian curator. Miran Mohar—a Slovenian artist and member of the IRWIN group—shares his personal view of, and his experiences in, the Kosovo art scene, while Szegin Boynik's essay critically discusses "The Subjectivity of Art against the Objectivity of the Nation."

Music has always played an important role in the Kosovo art scene. It was probably just a matter of time before a group of artists would start Tetris, an artist-run space in Prishtina, which over the years has served not only as a concert venue but also as a place for exhibitions and film screenings. In his text, Alsuh Gashi examines Tetris up close.

Charles Esche writes about the National Gallery of Kosovo during Erzen Shkololli's directorship, a period defined by the drive to update the institution and to draw the attention of international curators to the local scene. This period peaked in 2013, with Kosovo's first contribution to the Venice Biennale by Petrit Halilaj (curated by Kathrin Rhomberg), followed two years later by Flaka Haliti (curated by Nicolaus Schafhausen). Kathrin Rhomberg and Vanessa Joan Müller write about these two presentations, which would turn out to be important stepping stones for the young art scene of Kosovo on its way to international visibility and recognition.

Most recently, artistic interest has shifted towards language, poetry, and gender, as well as sociopolitical issues and the deployment of activist interventions, such as those of the HAVEIT collective. In short statements, they contribute their reflections on nationalisms, the oppression of women, and the lack of tolerance for the LGBT community and its manifestations.

Cathrin Mayer surveys the subculture and the future of the Kosovo art scene in a dialogue with Astrit Ismaili and Dardan Zhegrova, whose practices in performance art and poetry unfold through a queer subjectivity.

This collection of essays is published in the context of the tranzit.at Glossary Series which aims to encourage reflection on possible new and different approaches to creating common knowledge, more in sync with our time than the prevalent epistemological models, focusing on the new global conditions—and on the fact that we require more equality in creating knowledge under these conditions—as well as the need to redefine artistic geographies so that they can attune themselves to this new situation.

Contemporaneity, which started with the fall of the communist regimes and the accelerated processes of globalization, is characterized also by initiatives against hegemonic narratives and the existing dominant systems of knowledge. The series and this book also propose to detect a new, more horizontal dynamic in creating knowledge; not just any dynamic, however, but one that looks for the emancipatory potential of variously produced knowledge and its diverse forms of organization, primarily those excluded from the dominant systems.

Notes on Contemporary Art in Kosovo offers insight through various perspectives on the latest fundaments of artistic developments and further fosters reflection on how a local, prospering scene continuously raises new questions, and addresses undiscovered topics, hand in hand with the region's historical struggles in a search for identity while building/being the youngest state within Europe.

Katharina Schendl and
Georg Schollhammer (head of tranzit.at)

SUCCESSFULLY BROKE!

UNDER (CULTURAL) CONSTRUCTION

Vesa Sahatçiu

It is a challenge to summarize the various elements and apparatuses that have been constructing Kosovar culture since the end of the 1999 war. Therefore, I have decided to look at the visual arts arena, which, in my view, is not only constructing our culture, but also functioning as a miniature model that mimics the larger processes of our cultural/social shifts and developments.

Modernism

Kosovo's story of modern art begins after World War II with the founding of the University of Prishtina and its Academy of Fine Arts (1972–1974). This signaled the emergence of the first academic art current in the country that was based on modernist ideas. The art of this time (sculpture and painting) shows a mixture of folkloric and ethnological motifs and subject matter, combined with modernist ideas about art and modernist pictorial stylization. The best examples of such a combination are the paintings of Muslim Mulliqi, considered a representative painter of the time. In a text published in the catalogue for his 1979 solo exhibition, he states, "I cannot separate myself from my home, from the people that lived and created there." He then adds, "I think that a work that is honest and true is also contemporary, because today there is such freedom that the artist can paint an apple his own way—that is how he sees it, and how he feels it."[1]

This statement depicts the doctrine behind the work of the first generation of modern artists, as well as the ideas upon which the academy and its curriculum were founded. Such a mode of art making quickly became the criteria for academic art.

What becomes problematic later on is the lack of effort to reassess and eventually renew the criteria and curriculum, as well as the academy's closed attitude to new currents in art—such as conceptual art, performance art, etc. Furthermore, unlike in Belgrade, Zagreb, and Ljubljana—where dynamic artistic and student activity outside the academy was taking place, such as through Student Cultural Centre (SKC) activities in Belgrade from the mid-'70s onwards—in Prishtina, there were very little if any such activities, and the academy remained unaffected by the new trends in art. Instead, a strong obedience to the academy prevailed. In fact, during the '70s and '80s in Kosovo there was no strong subculture of rebellion against established artistic values (though it briefly appeared in the music scene with rock and new wave in the mid-'80s.)

A new wave in visual arts appeared halfway through the '90s, following the violent annexation of Kosovo in 1989 and the closing of all Albanian cultural and educational institutions.[2] During this time, a feeling of anti-academism, as well as the style and form of art it promoted, developed into a new art current that was being presented in alternative spaces, such as cafés and private galleries like the Dodona Gallery. Established notions of what constitutes art began to be questioned in such spaces. Abstract paintings appear for the first time in these alternative spaces; these do not use paint and canvas as their medium but everyday objects with an altered function. Such works were soon declared to be "nihilistic" and "anti-art."[3] It is interesting to note that although these activities were significant for the Kosovo arts, academics undervalued them as being a mere manifestation of Kosovo's political and social crisis. The tendency was perceived as a general decadence that would eventually subside once the context changed.

In 2004, five years after the NATO intervention, the academy remains unaltered. The curriculum is still the same. Another reason for dissatisfaction with art and culture is that, since the end of the 1999 war, there have been no attempts to place the artistic current in a historical perspective in order to bring it to an end, make it self-critical, and make others aware of its importance in the development of Kosovar art. Even prior to the ten-year Milošević regime and 1999 war, art historians did not undertake ambitious attempts to record and examine the important stream developing in visual arts (1960 to the 1980s), which had radically changed the visual arts in Kosovo. Even if this documentation exists, it is either lost or scattered around former Yugoslavia.

Postwar Fever, Us and Them

The relationship between Us and the Other, the other being the West, is important when examining conditions in the art domain—just as it is important in the whole political and cultural construction for Kosovo.

It is understandable that we use the West to measure almost everything. The same applies to the arts. In fact, all of the Eastern European bloc faces the same situation. The West has had a monopoly on values and criteria over most of the world for centuries. The West represents the ultimate values of art and culture, since it owns the most competent institutions and boasts the strongest art market. Often, such values are even of a self-criticizing nature. In fact, no other culture, existing under the banner of democracy and multiculturalism, has been more successful at promoting art that is critical toward its own foundations. Such art is even essential to the institution of art's own survival—it is the occasional antidote in moments when Western art reaches its peak, boredom sets in, or when such culture must punish itself, either out of instinctive sadomasochistic tendencies or merely as a means of feeling. This is where WE come in. This we, however, has not always been us. The door opened only recently—after 1999 to be more precise. Before us, there was the Orient. Thus Manet's and Toulouse-Lautrec's flat paintings; thus Gauguin's exotic paintings; thus Matisse's *Joy of Life*; thus Picasso's mask-like faces in *Les Demoiselles d'Avignon*. Today, being from the Balkans is exotic—is like being from the Other East.

Such a condition, created by existing power relations, determines our relationship with the West as well as our perception of it. Firstly, in the guardian relationship of superiority and inferiority, the West is the guardian and the all-knowing and value-setting motor; we are the children striving to live up to the values set by our guardian. Secondly, it is a relationship of difference or of *otherness*. They are the Other that we seek to become (at the institutional level), while we are the Other against whom they maintain their self-identity and onto which they experiment—consider, for instance, the eight standards Kosovo had to fulfill in order to become an independent state. The Albanian majority faces continuous pressure to be "politically correct"—in the pressure for superficial tolerance toward Serb minorities, for example. If such pressures are disputed for belonging to the family of "political correctness," I would only argue that the tolerance demanded at this stage and in this state of affairs can only be acted out—thus existing only as a cover-up.

This results in a democracy and stability merely based on spectacle and artificiality. It is based, basically, on what "political correctness" has come to mean. In 2003, the increasing global uniformity we face due to the new age of "multinational capitalism"[4] ensures that otherness functions only on the bases of such uniformity. Therefore, you can be different as long as you comply with the so-called rules of being different; you can be different only as long as you speak through mediums and processes that are uniform. Or to put it in uniform words, you can express your particularity only through the mediums and the processes that have been made universal and acceptable

Even though the East is active in constructing its own identity, the fear still exists that it will fall into the trap of identifying and presenting itself through the West's projection. The already classic example of this pitfall is the 1995 film by Emir Kusturica, *Underground*, which Slavoj Žižek discussed in his essay "Multiculturalism, or, The Cultural Logic of Multinational Capitalism" (1997).

In Žižek's words, what the film "offers to the Western liberal gaze is exactly what this gaze wants to see in the Balkan war—the spectacle of a timeless, incomprehensible, mythical circuit of passions."[5] In big European exhibitions, there is the fear that the East is being presented according to preconceived Western ideas and notions. There is always the fear that this difference is expected from the Eastern artist. There is always the fear, as mentioned in the beginning, that the East is there only because there isn't much else left to be exploited. There is always the fear that since initially, "liberal 'tolerance' condones the folklorist Other (who is) deprived of its substance," their presence in big exhibitions is "like a multitude of 'ethnic cuisines' in a contemporary megalopolis."[6]

Such issues, directly or indirectly, concern some of the young artists who, through their work, question the assigned otherness and what they seemingly are supposed to represent.[7] One such artist is Jakup Ferri. In the video *Save Me, Help Me* (2003), Ferri, in a very honest and simple way, reveals the relationship between West and East. The artist frames himself as the stereotypical Eastern artist—talented but alienated since he lives in the margins.

In the video, he shows samples of his work and calls upon foreign curators to promote his practice so as to finally save him. The deliberate process of acting out his assigned role, one of the marginalized Eastern artist, reveals the synthetic constructions of this otherness by making it banal, and thus freeing the artist from it.

But there is another twist to Ferri's work. Or to put it in a universal discourse, in this work, as in almost everything else, there is the other side of the coin. Allow me to state the following: Ferri "plays" a real role in his work. He is a poor artist, from a poor part of the world, who seeks to go abroad in order to succeed as an artist. Such is his reality. He is, paradoxically, the cliché of the Eastern artist. At the same time, being aware of the assigned role by Western multiculturalists, he acts out his own role deliberately. As such, he reveals the assigned positions of both sides (Eastern poor artist; Western all-powerful curators) and openly points at the means to success—Eastern artist + Western curator = success. As such, Ferri does not accept his role passively. Instead, he tries to disclose his superficial role within the power relations between East and West.

Us and Ourselves

The postwar period in Kosovo generally is associated with further decay of the academy and the emergence and development of alternative spaces. Such spaces have been created by individuals engaged in the counter-wave movement of the mid-to late '90s, who also helped shape a new generation of visual artists by creating a new, dynamic art scene that is internationally known.

The decay of the academy, as with most "state" institutions, has been largely the result of the ten-year Milošević regime, which brought to a halt any institutional development. Meanwhile, complete isolation from the outside world has led to a lack of information, and thus prevented intellectual development of the region's intellectual circles. This "un-natural" stagnation in virtually all fields has made it difficult to get back on track. Furthermore, the ten-year period of parallel governance in Kosovo—besides preserving a sense of civil society, security, and organization—gave birth to incompetent "professionals" who insist on the eligibility of their positions within the "state" institution. Such attitudes have contributed to the decadence of institutions. At the same time, promising individuals have been pushed into alternative spaces outside the institutional realm.

Therefore, I would conclude that the widespread anti-academism among the younger generation is not due to a sudden disbelief in the institutional system or a rebellion toward its institutionalized values. Rather, it is due to the lack of any valid criteria or value within these institutions. It is a rebellion against their total decadence. In other words, the anti-academism that we are experiencing calls for stronger institutions with up-to-date curricula, and a strong intellectual and academic body that is able to offer insight and the space for alternative work to be made.

First published in *Arta* in 2003.

1 Alltene Taipi, *Muslim Mulliqi: Retrospektiva 1953-1979*, Gallery of Arts, Prishtina 1979.

2 Shkëlzen Maliqi, *Beyond: The New Art of Kosovo*, Center for Contemporary Arts, Belgrade 1998.

3 Ibid.

4 Slavoj Žižek, "Multiculturalism, or, The Cultural Logic of Multinational Capitalism," in: Zdenka Badovinac / Peter Weibel, *Arteast 2000+. The Art of Eastern Europe. A Selection of Works for the International and National Collection of Moderna galerija Ljubljana*, Vienna / Bolzano 2001.

5 Ibid.

6 Ibid.

7 Badovinac refers to Oleg Kulik and the IRWIN group as artists who are critical of their otherness. Zdenka Badovinac, "Body and the East," in *Body and the East: From the 1960's to the Present*, exhibition catalogue, Moderna galerija/Museum of Modern Art, Ljubljana 1998.

SHADOWING SEXISM!

CROSSROADS OF KOSOVO'S NEW ART

Shkëlzen Maliqi

A Short Narrative

The contemporary visual arts scene in Kosovo emerged and developed rapidly sometime around the mid-90s, only to reach its peak during 2003–4 when a group of authors from Kosovo, mostly from the younger generations, managed to penetrate the global art scene. Visits by renowned curators and the participation of Kosovar artists in explorative exhibitions about fictional "Balkan Arts" (such as Harald Szeemann's *Blood & Honey—The Future's in the Balkans*, Vienna, 2003; and René Block's *In the Gorges of the Balkans: A Report*, Kassel, 2003) immediately marked new names as representatives of the art of this region. In fact, René Block returned to Kosovo and told a local weekly magazine, *Java*, that in Kosovo he had discovered "the avant-garde of Balkan contemporary arts."[1]

With the exception of Sisley Xhafa and Petrit Halilaj, who had managed to succeed in the West on their own, the most renowned names of this new art scene included Sokol Beqiri, Erzen Shkololli, Jakup Ferri, Flaka Haliti, Lulzim Zeqiri, Dren Maliqi, Fitore Isufi / Koja, Driton Hajredinaj, Alban Muja, Vigan Nimani, Albert Heta and Merita Harxhi Koci. These artists especially excelled at making remarkable video art pieces. The Slovenian curator Nadja Zgonik said that contemporary Kosovar video art is among the most accomplished in Europe.[2]

Others who play an important role in Kosovo's art scene are Mehmet Behluli, an artist and professor, and the theorists and critics Shkëlzen Maliqi, Sezgin Boynik, and Vesa Sahatçiu. Kosovar art activities have taken place mostly at EXIT Gallery in Peja (2004–6), more recently at Rizoma (2006) and Stacion (2006 till today) in Prishtina, as well at the National Gallery of Kosovo (while Erzen Shkololli was director, 2011–15).

Compared to other parts of former Yugoslavia, where contemporary art movements existed throughout the years of communism, the new art in Kosovo seems as if it has sprung out of nowhere. Sezgin Boynik has published an essay saying that the beginning of contemporary art in Kosovo was influenced by reading and studying the book *Art Now,* published by Taschen.[3] A similar movement can be found in the Kurdish region of Turkey. Apart from being "lost provinces," the artistic circles of Kosovo and Diyarbakir "surprisingly" produced a new wave of talents who used new mediums and expressed themselves in modern, or even postmodern language.

The similarities between the Kosovar and Diyarbakir scenes in terms of aesthetics and substance became visible in a joint exhibition in Croatia, *M'vyn ndrim radikal – I Need Radical Change,* curated by the What, How and for Whom (WHW) curatorial collective.[4] The curators claimed that artists from the two "provinces" represent authentic and original honesty. What they represented, in fact, was the East in general.

Referring to Kosovo's art scene as "avant-garde," the curator Edi Muka cynically claimed that Eastern artists are in fact "new proletarians in the world of art" who have no prospect of competition with mainstream Western cultures.[5] Given this attitude, claims of "discoveries"—that the art scene *emerged out of nowhere*—were bound to face criticism. Szeemann, Block, and the others were accused of treating art from the region as an "exotic product" from the postcolonial cultural market.

But now that Western criticism and curatorial practices have turned their spotlight elsewhere, Kosovar contemporary art, as well as art from the East in general, is faced with a genuine challenge: being in the desperate position of the proletarian needing to sustain the domestic scene without help from the West.

During its peak, the Kosovar art scene received support from many global foundations. Throughout the '90s, the scene was mainly assisted by the Open Society Foundation (The Soros Foundation). From 2003 to 2006, Germany's Kulturstiftung des Bundes made capital investments in the scene as part of its *Relations* project. For a decade Pro Helvetia was also a heavy supporter of the Kosovo art scene (2001–11). While the ever-expanding art scene is witnessing the emergence of new trends (lately even a return to painting), as well as new names, it also has started to suffocate due to lack of funds and the lack of an art market.

In the 1990s, following the apartheid imposed by the Serbian regime, Kosovars had become accustomed to creating parallel lives and scenes that functioned free of external interference. Having spent two decades opposing the Serbian regime and its imposed reality, Kosovo's contemporary art scene was not concerned as much about the lack of support from Kosovar institutions—such institutions were also "parallel" and "outside of the system."

The Two Art Scenes

After the war and the establishment of the international administration in Kosovo, the two art scenes continue to coexist separately. One considers itself the "official" scene, because it works from tradition, receives institutional support, and has an academy and galleries. The other scene functions separately from institutions, in improvised spaces, with informal schools and through methods that seem subversive. The latter scene is more creative and dynamic; it quickly managed to have a presence in the big European exhibitions. Its artists are considered curious, courageous, reflective, and critical toward the real problems of society and the place art seizes within it.

Meanwhile, the "official" art scene, which proclaims itself to be a follower of the finest Kosovar traditions, has not found an answer to the challenges of our time. The same holds even for the most qualitative art produced by the modernist generation. The late doyen, Kosovar painter Muslim Mulliqi,[6] is a clear example. His work during the '90s, although highly expressive, became increasingly introspective, gloomy, and depressive.

The two art scenes do not have a common nest or mediator. The truth is that institutional art transferred itself into politics and ideology, as if to follow the famous saying: *At a time of war, there is no place for art.* It was no coincidence that Ibrahim Rugova, a writer, would become a political leader as well as Kosovo's first president following liberation from Serbia and the establishment of an international administration. Meanwhile, the non-institutional and subversive art scene appears patriotic, in the sense that it irradiates substantial artistic resistance toward repression—and after 1999, it addressed the need for the radicalization of contemporary art and its practices.

Although the extremist mouthpieces from the "official art scene" made allegations against the new scene—even charging it with betraying tradition and "national values"—the new art led the way into subversiveness against any occupation or opposition to freedom. It did this using the most contemporary of means and a language that was understood well beyond Kosovo's borders.

The defensiveness and dryness of the official art on the one hand, and the penetration and creativity of the new art scene on the other, cannot maintain the status of being two parallel realities. These two scenes face a decisive confrontation. The alternative scene seeks to legitimize its presence and influence. The most essential issue will be the opportunity to use public funds, which so far have been monopolized by official art. Kosovo's unresolved political status has also offered a pretext for avoiding internal confrontations. However, after Kosovo proclaimed independence on February 17, 2008, this can no longer hold. The contemporary art scene has benefited from Western "neocolonial" funds, even when such funds helped artists run away to the West. However, those artists who wish to remain in Kosovo now know that more dangerous than this "neocolonialism" is the prospect of their colonization by the past and narrow-minded cultural policies and traditions.

Another battle has been conducted in Kosovo around the inclusion of contemporary art practices in the Academy of Arts of Prishtina University. For many years, conservative professors refused to accept the teaching and practice of performance, installations, video art, and so on. Only after a long-standing commitment to this issue by Mehmet Behluli and Sisely Xhafa was a new Department of Conceptual Art established in 2012.

The heartburn of the conservative spirit in art criticism towards the new forms of expression in Kosovo has intensified during the last decade. Whether in various painting exhibitions, in opinion pieces published in the press, or in frequent discussions about art, traditionalist circles are sounding the alarm bells on the general risk that the penetration of a new and different kind of art brings. They dislike the fact that the new art is increasingly "occupying" some of the very few Kosovo art institutions; they say that this represents injustice toward "genuine art," that these experiments of suspicious quality are favored because they are foreign, foreign, but that they do not coincide with Kosovo's genuine artistic tradition, the "spirit of our soil."[7]

It is a fact that what has occurred lately in Kosovo is a division within the visual arts scene, more open than in other art scenes, into two main paths of artistic practice and organization, one of which can conditionally be dubbed *traditionalist*, and the other *innovative* or *explorative.*

It is also a fact that the new art, the explorative and experimental type, not only due to its apparent courage to demolish taboos and established forms of expression, but also due to its quality and the success it has achieved outside of Kosovo, is strongly challenging the traditional and adherent art of painting, sculpture, graphics, and design, the concepts and the taste of which remain deeply and recalcitrantly conservative. The phenomena of conservative worldviews being challenged is not uniquely Kosovar, nor Albanian, since it is an occurrence that continues to happen even today in the most developed countries—conservative establishments reacting to avant-garde provocations that shatter and deny established artistic traditions and values. Furthermore, there is nothing special or worrisome in the confrontational polarization between artistic practices (we are still in its initial phase). It is a confrontation that lacks delicacy and mutual tolerance and is nourished by a division that insists on WE and THEM as exclusive and refutable categories ("Are you with US or with THEM?"; "Are you with genuine art or worthless art?").[8]

There is nothing surprising in this, since such divisions are found, more or less, in all places and ages. Rather, what appears odd is the fact that Kosovo and Albania did not have these confrontations and competitions between generations and different artistic movements earlier (and when they occured, they were dingy and repressed until they became unnoticeable). Therefore, the phenomena at hand could paradoxically be described as a kind of normalization of the city's artistic and cultural life. At last, here are signs that the Kosovo art scenes are shaking themselves up, awakening from their provincial lethargy and sleep. Something is happening, something is being contested and defended; competitions, debates, conflicts, contestations, etc. are being forewarned and requested. Not as something negative, but as proof of the fact that, in these contradictions, we show dynamic development potentials, sources of liveliness and life.

Within this expanded and quite elastic argument I want to express my understanding for the existence of conservative taste and criticism. It can, in fact, be useful if articulated properly and if built upon already proven traditional values and concepts. But the problem with the conservative critique in the Kosovo context is that it is being expressed in an overbold manner, it is uncultivated and without finesse—it is being expressed only through growls and accusations that do not show any sign of power or positive conviction. Most of the adherents of this critique show only concepts that are quite primitive.

The conservative arguments are in most cases banal, contradictory, and illogical. They refute the new art in an *en bloc* manner. They say: "New art is not real art, it is anti-art"; "New art is something with no value, only a pale copy of experiments in Western contemporary art"; "All over the world, this sort of art is considered problematic and degenerated"; "For us, it is a foreign art, it does not suit and cannot be part of the tradition, mentality, taste, and real needs of our environment," etc.

The conservative critique consists first of all in attempts to unjustly take away the Kosovar and Albanian artists' right try out new forms of expression (video, installation, etc.) the way their colleagues around the world do; in fact, the artist does so not because he or she wants to, but because he or she needs to. According to the conservatives, Albanian and Kosovar culture should remain an oasis of established traditional values and forms of art. Quite simply, according to them, you are an artist if you paint or make sculptures.

Usually this concept is argued and seeks support in idealized artistic and national values—based on an idea not quite articulated that suggests the existence of a *genuine national art*. In fact, the conservatives don't know what they're talking about when they say that "artists should cultivate and create first and foremost *our* art, the art of the *national spirit*." They only say, in a generalized way, that the prime inspiration for the art of today should be—the art of tradition.

But if we were to analyze, even superficially, what is meant by, and what is the corpus of the art of national tradition that conservative critics have in mind, the argument would be a mystification of its own kind. "The art of tradition," keeping in mind the exclusiveness that is given to this notion, would fit in its imagined frame almost none of our great artists in the Albanian art tradition—take any of them: medieval Byzantine master Onufri (16th century), Abdurrahim Buza, Sali Shijaku, Odhise Paskali, Muslim Mulliqi, Agim Çavdarbasha, or any other modern visual artist. None of the above-mentioned artists could be apprehended as a real artist without acknowledging the many references, schools, and influences taken from international art and artists! Furthermore, if one part of traditional art is excluded—the one that substantially and thematically is associated with historical figures and events—then the other part, perhaps representing the overwhelming majority of traditional Albanian visual arts, could not, without any consequences, be separated from the influences of foreign visual arts. Why can't the artist be influenced by the world today if artists in the past experienced limitless influence from the "foreign" mainstream arts of their age?

In literature, the criterion of the national could in fact be used, to a certain extent, as a point of reference in defining "national literature," since language is truly a "uniqueness" that can actually build, however artificially, the "jargons of authenticity" and the autochthony of the words and artistic writings of a nation. But which would be the pure and rooted form of Kosovar or Albanian visual tradition? Did the Albanians by any chance discover a specific visual "language"? Did they discover the authentic Albanian scene in the non-geographic understanding of the word? Is there something like an art of portraiture with an Albanian specificity to it? Other questions could be raised as well, questions that derive from the conservative insistence on the necessity to follow "our tradition."

What Is Meant by Traditional Art?
We could discuss the issue more concretely. What should be seen as, for example, the purely Albanian content, obligatory for the new generation, in the art of someone like Muslim Mulliqi? There is no doubt that Mulliqi is an artist of the highest caliber and that Kosovo owes him a lot. This debt to him is not settled by giving away the annual Mulliqi Prize, inaugurated in 2008, an event that upset traditionalists and conservatives, since the prize was given to two young artists "who ignore tradition and do conceptual art"! Should we appreciate in Mulliqi's works only his motifs and themes (for example, painting *kulla*s, traditional Albaninan fortress or tower houses) or should we in fact see that his paintings are more complex, more reflexive, and that they have pictorial values which are not conditioned by local tradition, but rather reflect a mastery captured from global traditions, like Fajumi's encaustic portraits from the Hellenistic period (323–31 BC) or from modern European and ex-Yugoslavian paintings?

Since the issue at hand here is Mulliqi, I would like tell the conservatives that they shouldn't bore the public by talking about his national values, because the most important thing in his work, the most original thing, is his genius, his hand and his individual mastery. This is combined also with the spirit that is reflected in his work—an interlacing of the dilemmas of his time and age, where, among other things, communism and existentialism were very influential ideologies that were unavoidable for his generation in the former Yugoslavia, and which were of course transformed into figurative visions. In his last phase, the old Mulliqi invests a boyish energy into finding images that reflect universality, enriched by an almost religious atmosphere, on the one hand celebrating the immortal and perpetual beauty of the woman, and on the other treating the immortal beauty of nature and its scenery. By doing so, he left a melancholic testament of his participation in the wonder and marvel of life as his legacy. He expresses the visions of a person taken aback by beauty, as the only discernable proof that brings us near to the divine, to the heavenly.

Another example that proves the absurdity of the insistence on "rooted" and "national" painting would be the works of Tahir Emra,[9] whom I suppose the conservatives would also like to portray as a model of "genuine art." There is no doubt that Emra too is one of the bards of Kosovar painting. But, if in his work we would look for the aforementioned autochthonous national values, we could hardly find them in crystal clear form, and could therefore hardly see it as the prescribed model. Emra is a skillful painter, but his work is rooted and original to the same extent that it owes a debt to the schools and teachers he has had—and only a few of them are from our own cultural soil. If we were to be malicious, we would say that Emra's teachers were the artists of a school of tardy Slavic modernism, a school that itself shows traces of the influences of global modernism. If the totally absurd conservative nationalist logic of acceptance versus exclusion would be respected in its entirety, then Emra would not pass the basic test of authenticity, and he too would have to go through the purgatory of removing from his work the influence of "Slavic" paintings! But of course, it is understood that this is a foolish argument—an argument that, when developed in its entirety, boomerangs negatively on conservative criticism itself.

The paradox of conservative critique is that, in traditional art, it values objectively more the form and the established medium of expression (painting, sculpture, etc.), than the content that expresses the idea of the obligatory national spirit in art. On the other hand, it becomes entirely blind to the content and the spirit of new art, which in fact deals with actuality, politics, the fate of the nation, the tragedies we have experienced, national symbols, etc. It does so only because these subjects are treated in untraditional mediums of expression (video, installation, performance, etc). Furthermore, I would bet any conservative that the new art proportionally uses (of course, in its own way) more of the motifs and themes of tradition, folklore, the symbols, characters, and events in our history, than traditional art has done so far. In other words, if we were to look at it closely, in the works of Sokol Beqiri, Erzen Shkololli, Sisli Xhafa, Petrit Halilaj, Mehmet Behluli, Albert Heta, Jakup Ferri, Dren Maliqi, Flaka Haliti, Lulëzim Zeqiri, Merita Harxhi Koci, Driton Hajredini, and other young artists who favor new forms of expression, we would find more of the national content so much adored by conservatives than in the works of traditional artists.

Setting aside the issue of evaluations dependent upon knowledge and taste, no one can deny the fact that visual art in Kosovo has never been more engaged than today. At the same time, Kosovar visual arts have now penetrated the international stage and been evaluated more positively there than ever before.

1 “Ne Prishtinë takova avangardën e re të Ballkanit,” *Java*, No. 5 (July, 2003): 8. See also from René Block: “On one of my last trips to the Balkans, I came across an exhibition at the Academy of Fine Arts in Prishtina, which featured very young Kosovo artists, some of whom were still students. The Albanian curator Edi Muka had compiled the astonishing show. Considering the prevailing political context, some of the works were so outrageously impudent, cunning and humorous that I was left speechless.” From the catalogue of the exhibition. *In the Gorges of the Balkans: A Report*, Kassel 2003.

2 Vesa Sahatçiu, “Identiteti është dialog: Intervistë me kuratoren Nadja Zgonik,” *Java*, Arta supplement No. 3 (March 2004): p. 4.

3 “One of the most influential books for the contemporary art scene of Kosovo was the book ‘Art Now’ published by Taschen in 2002. The young Kosovo art students were learning from it how to think, how to see and how to say things as contemporary artists.” Sezgin Boynik “Cultural Roots of Contemporary Art in Kosovo,” http://radical.temp.si/reader/Sezgin.pdf.

4 Galeria Nova, Zagreb, 2004.

5 René Block, *In the Gorges of the Balkans: A Report*, catalogue of the exhibition, Kunsthalle Fridericianum, Kassel 2003.

6 Muslim Mulliqi, 1934–1998

7 Uran Limani, “Një opinion për ‘Artin përnjime’ dhe ‘Artin pa vlerë,’” *Java*, Arta Supplement, Nos. 8–9 (October 2004): p. 8.

8 Uran Limani, “This kind of modern art is worthless… I don’t like this art. My art is painting…” Ibid., 7.

9 Tamir Emra, born 1938 in Peja.

WHEN FATHER WEPT, MOTHER WASHED MY EYES

JUMPING STRAIGHT INTO THE PRESENT

Shkëlzen Maliqi
in conversation with *Edi Muka*

SHKËLZEN MALIQI *While preparing this book on contemporary art in Kosovo, we have been reminded that almost since the beginning of new art emerging in Kosovo, from the late '90s until you moved to Sweden in 2005, you were one of the people who knew its scene the best. The almost simultaneous awakenings of the two scenes—of explorative new art and the use of new media in Albania and Kosovo—have had their own particularities. How do you look back on this period today and what were the significant differences, if there were any, between the art that was being created in Albania and Kosovo?*

As you mentioned, the awakening of the contemporary art scenes in Kosovo and Albania coincided in time and to some extent in circumstances, and I think we have more resemblances than differences. Albania had gone through the troubled years of regime change, during which a rapid shift of positions and hierarchies took place in the art scene. Within a short time span, between years 1994 and 1999, an even younger generation of artists emerged, defined by the attempt to engage with the present and try to articulate the events taking place in Albania during those years of radical change. They were also the first to test new forms of expression that prevailed over the traditional tools of sculpture and painting. This generation and these tendencies emerged most distinctly after 1997, which was one of the most traumatic and troublesome years, one that would delineate the new trends in political developments in the country.

On the other hand, Kosovo, almost at the same time and at the same pace, entered the most intense phase of developments that followed a decade of parallel social life and culminated with the war and destruction, displacement of the population, and the NATO bombing in 1999. Just like in Albania, a new generation of Kosovar artists, totally shaped by the experiences of those events, began their efforts to articulate them aesthetically. So in a way, with or without their intent, the artistic creativity of both scenes towards the end of the ’90s, years that coincide with what you define as an awakening, were conditioned and shaped by trauma, violence, and war—and the shock and collapse of social structures. On the other hand, they were also shaped by the transformation and opening of a new horizon of desires, opportunities, and enthusiasm, which served as the only fuel for the engine of society, enabling the avoidance of the total collapse of its social fabric.

In addition to geopolitical developments, there are some other similar features that I can list below. In the formal/aesthetic sense, almost all artists who somehow became part of these developments (we cannot talk about artists’ movements in their truest sense) began to look for new means of expression, especially through video, but also installation, collage, site-specific interventions, and occasionally, performance. However, in the art-historical aspect, both scenes are characterized by a lack of links and references to the legacy of modernity in art, as a result of the long isolation both Albania and Kosovo were subject to, albeit for different reasons. So, in a way, in an effort to bridge the historical gap, the artists of both scenes adopted a form of “leaping” or “jumping” straight into the present as the most appropriate tactic to articulate their time.

Another feature characteristic of the time was the emigration of some of the artists, whose work was now marked by their new global position. This coincided with the great interest shown by the Western world and art institutions, especially in Europe, toward the emerging art scenes of Eastern Europe. But while almost all the other Eastern European countries had enjoyed some kind of autonomy and had experienced forms of modernity and artistic movements, no one had any idea what had happened in Albania and Kosovo. From this point of view, both countries were objects of curiosity as compared to other Eastern European art scenes.

Finally, a summary feature that goes beyond the Albanian and Kosovar scenes, and which we should not forget about, is that the developments that coincide with the articulation of contemporary art expressions in Kosovo and Albania are part of a wider and similar spectrum of developments in more or less the entire periphery of countries that emerged from the former Eastern Bloc. This framework does not explain, but creates the historical references to understand why these developments are focused on identity issues (in Kosovo we cannot yet talk about national identity issues but rather a vacuum in this respect), something also typical for many countries of the former Soviet Union, expressed through the universal language of contemporary art. On the other side of this coin, we also see a lack of critical analysis of these "integration" phenomena in the global contemporary art scene and, with the passing of the years, the weakening of the historical premises that gave rise to the respective generation of artists (i.e., social transformations, war, and the powerful experiences of events that anyone could relate to). The result was that artists attained their social position more through external interest than through interconnecting or working with the local public.

In my opinion, as far as difference or distinctness is concerned, we find it on two planes. On the first plane we find the particular subjects that artists treat in their works. They are closely related to the particularities and histories of the two territories, which until then had been completely separate from one another. The second plane has to do with the specific historical particularities of the development of the two scenes. The Albanian scene really came out of the darkness, from an unprecedented isolation and almost total ignorance of classical and late modernity in terms of experiences, tendencies, or artistic movements, both in the West and in Eastern Europe. Meanwhile, in Kosovo, having lived for many decades within the framework of the former Yugoslavia enabled at least educational opportunities in the big centers and the possibility of contact and acquaintance with the major movements of modernity. This is also noticeable in the approach of Kosovar artists and creators toward all cultural fields: music, theater, visual arts, film, and literature.

SH.M. *By the end of the '90s, the affirmation of new art in Kosovo, in the sense of the emergence and recognition that such a thing even exists within the conditions of apartheid we were living and working under at the time, was the exhibition that we organized in June 1997 in Belgrade, at the Center for Cultural Decontamination. This exhibition, which was presented with an Albanian title in the middle of Belgrade, echoed throughout the region. After a few months, Sokol Beqiri and Mehmet Behluli were invited to the Cetinje Biennale, where we met Edi Rama and Ornela Vorpsi, who were also participants. At that point, you were informed that in Kosovo a new art was emerging and you invited several artists to the first international Onufri Award exhibition, held at the National Gallery of Arts in Tirana. What do you remember about these first contacts with Kosovar artists?*

E.M. My first more complete encounter with the work of Kosovar artists took place in somewhat random circumstances, and it was thanks to Lala Meredith-Vula. In the second half of the 1990s, which were very dynamic and enthusiastic years at the Academy of Arts in Tirana, Lala held a photography course. One evening as we were sitting in a cafe (a pastime which still prevails as the main form of inter-societal exchange in Albania and Kosovo), Lala showed me an album of photographs of interventions a group of Kosovar artists had done in the ruins of the bazaar in Peja. This aroused my curiosity and I wanted to know more about what was going on in Kosovo. I had already started to work internationally, bringing the work of Albanian artists into different contexts and exhibitions, but also presenting it to visiting curators from abroad, who during those years were visiting Albania in numbers.

Given the sensibilities and characteristics of the works of artists from both sides of the border that I described above, I felt the responsibility to introduce the work of the Kosovar artists to the international, professional circles of art.

These first exchanges would be followed by frequent collaborations within the framework of various exhibitions and publications, held in Albania or elsewhere. Naturally, the cooperation was initially between a group of artists belonging to the pre-war generation of Kosovo. Gradually, another generation of young artists began to flourish, giving rise to a slightly different research process but nevertheless linked to the legacy of the previous generation. This new research, in my opinion, shifted from close connection to the frantic experiences of the years during and after the war, which began to slowly fade from memory, towards issues of cultural identity, which I mentioned earlier in relation to global society, but also the history of art and culture, especially Western. Of course, the research premises were determined by the geopolitical situation of Kosovo at that time (the isolation, inability to travel, emigration etc.). But the treatment of the topics took a very individual approach, where each artist tried to build her/his own expression through history or personal experiences regarding these phenomena. In general terms, I can say that the works of this generation transmit bouts of irony and humor, and to some extent absurdism, to an even greater degree than what we could have encountered in the works of the previous generation.

Another thing I can mention, in these first two generations, is the lack of efforts to stimulate and give space to female artists, and here I also blame myself for the way I approached both the Albanian and Kosovar art scenes. However, I must say that the presence and participation of female artists in Kosovo was more visible than in Albania, and fortunately this imbalance has changed somewhat in recent years.

Have you been following the most recent art developments in Kosovo? How would you assess Kosovar art in general?

E.M. As for the developments of the Kosovo scene today, I have to say that I haven't followed it as closely as I used to. However, through a small residency program that we continue to run in Tirana and ongoing exchanges with independent organizations, such as Stacion, or friends and artist colleagues in Kosovo, I have been able to keep up to a certain extent. I can say that I am pleased to note that there is now a deepening focus and research as well as reflection on the conditions of being part of the Kosovar society, along with the aesthetic articulation and challenging of political and social structures, especially patriarchal ones, and also poetic research into human relationships, etc. Moreover, I notice that there is a growing trend towards experimentation with performance, with interventions by the all-female collective HAVEIT, which stands out as a form of dynamic expression that creates often direct and radical confrontations in public space.

SH.M. *Albanian artists, as individual creators, operate all over the world. We have artists who have represented several countries; for instance, at the Venice Biennale, Sislej Xhafa has represented Albania, Italy, and Kosovo. We can thank the openness of today's art world for this artistic nomadism. But in the context of "globalization," is there room for something called "Albanian art"? I ask you this because in the past you have curated Albanian art exhibitions; for example,* Beautiful Strangers *in Berlin in 2001. How do you see the issue of Albanian art today? Can it be treated as a whole, or are there at least two separate scenes (Albania and Kosovo), that also have different forms of cooperation and interaction?*

E.M. Your question is interesting but also difficult to answer. During the period you refer to, there were prerequisites that made it possible to outline what was called the "Albanian art scene." On the one hand, paradoxically, this definition was framed to some extent by a curiosity coming from the outside about our scenes, a phenomenon that is obviously temporary, or rather, occasional. On the other hand, there was a mutual curiosity to discover each other after infinite decades of no contact or exchange. Finally, there are the thematic and formal similarities I mentioned above.

If we are talking about an Albanian art scene today, I think we need to adopt a global approach to the term "scene" and to specific geographic notions, such as "Albanian." This is about a tangible reality, which is not only typical of the "Albanian art scene." In short, a good deal of Albanian artists today, as you mentioned, live and work outside of Albania and Kosovo. Yet, the vast majority of them are connected to the local scene and their respective countries mainly through their work and the topics they deal with. In this sense, the Albanian scene surpasses the physical boundaries of the two countries. I think the time has come to do serious research on the development of the scene, which should culminate with special exhibitions. This should be taken over by art institutions, but in close dialogue with—and with the broad involvement of—the independent scene, which almost single-handedly carries the weight of responsibility for the scene's development.

This research, which should replace the already atrophied award-based events in both Kosovo and Albania, should be set up as agenda activities, with regular recurrences once every few years. Only in this way would it be possible to measure the pulse and observe the health or the existence of an Albanian art scene. We would also be able to observe the main trends and forms of expression. Until this pursuit is systematized, we will only have sporadic appearances of what can be called an Albanian scene.

On the other hand, if I tried to give a more direct answer to your question, I would say I think it is possible to outline the Albanian scene. I also think it is an interesting process, because despite the fact that the two separate scenes, both Kosovar and Albanian, do not have a systematic and structural exchange, somewhere at a subconscious level they are complementary to each other. For example, while the work of young artists in Albania is concerned with the impact of physical changes to the territory (especially in Tirana), reactions to political developments, and reflections on the history of the communist past, in the works of Kosovo artists we can observe a more poetic approach to human and family relationships, or a more open and sometimes radical confrontation with social structures that shape and dominate society. It is also interesting to observe the means of expression. In the works of Albanian artists, we see that video and photography, as well as a reemergence of painting, are dominant; while in Kosovo, apart from objects and installations, there is a widespread tendency to explore performance. But these are only quick thoughts, which need to be deepened through the research processes mentioned above.

SH.M. *One of your memorable descriptions of Albanian art was "permanent instability," due to the lack of institutions and supportive activities a developed art system needs. Do you think things have changed in this respect today?*

E.M. I used the term *Permanent Instability* as the title of the first international exhibition in Tirana, under the Onufri Prize in 1998. In fact, the term referred to the Balkans as a geopolitical area defined by instability, since that first exhibition focused on artists from the Balkan countries. In parenthesis, I would say that this term, sadly (or not) had a prophetic tinge to it, since today this condition has become the norm on a global level. At the time I used it, I was referring to the geopolitical situation the region was going through, which also affected the artistic scenes and cultural structures. Unfortunately, I have to say that there is still no change to these policy-making and funding structures in Kosovo and Albania, with a few exceptions, such as the commitment to participate in the art and architecture Venice Biennales—which sounds like a paradox when put in the context of the deficiencies we experience on the local level. The legal framework for supporting state or independent institutions is almost nonexistent, unchanged for many years, and does not reflect the dynamics of the scene's development.
In this sense, "instability" is what continues to characterize the scenes in both Albania and Kosovo. In recent years, the scenes have been enriched with new initiatives or by new research from those initiatives that have been operating for a long time. To some extent, I can say that now some attention is being paid by central institutions towards the activities of the

independent scene. But what poses a problem is the lack of long-term strategies and policies that would enable initiatives to develop programs and long-term regional or international exchanges, which would somewhat move us away from the culture of temporary—hence, unsustainable—projects, which in my opinion have already carried out their function and now can only undermine opportunities for many young people, artists, curators, or educators to work in the field of culture. These shortcomings also have a direct impact on relations with the public, in the sense that the lack of mediating programs through art educators has resulted in a significant decline in interest in art. Of course, it is society that suffers the consequences of not having these intermediate mechanisms, by becoming increasingly alienated not only from artistic experiences but also from the opportunity to build a different type of relationship with art, a relationship where the artist can directly contribute to larger processes such as community building and city development. So, in my opinion, the underlying problem is not simply that money for art and culture is missing, which is true, but there is also a lack of desire and political will to see art and culture as important cogs in our societal machine.

SH.M. *At documenta 14 (2017) we for the first time had more than decent representation of Kosovar art, including Sokol Beqiri, Agim Çavdarbasha, and the British-Kosovar artist Lala Meredith-Vula. In addition to this, documenta 14 also presented Edi Hila and a group of Albanian artists from the socialist realist period. I have the impression that at this point, at least in Kosovo, the "heroic" period of getting in step with the rest of the world has been concluded, since we are experiencing the affirmation of a new generation of artists who have a different sensibility and cultivate a different type of art, even when they deal with identity motifs, such as in the art of Petrit Halilaj, HAEVIT, or Flaka Haliti.*

E.M. I absolutely agree with you. I also think the “heroic” period is over and it is time for the “heroes” to engage in a process of contributing to the new art scene.

An example to admire is Adrian Paci’s initiative to turn his home into an “Art House” serving the entire artistic community of the city of Shkodra in Albania and beyond.

SHAVING PATRIARCHY!

IF WE DON'T ORGANIZE OURSELVES, OTHERS WILL DO IT FOR US

Miran Mohar

My involvement with Kosovo goes back a long way. While still a student in the 1980s, I joined the protests in solidarity with the inhabitants of what was then called the Autonomous Province of Kosovo and Metohija. With the exception of a few Albanian students in Ljubljana, I had no personal acquaintances in or from Kosovo. My source of reliable information about what was going on there in the late 1980s and early 1990s was my friend Goran Djordjević, whom I valued as an artist; his early art had a significant impact on both the Laibach and Irwin art collectives. Goran had moved from Kosovo to Belgrade in the late 1970s, but continued to teach at the Faculty of Architecture in Prishtina until 1991 (almost up to the time of the outbreak of war in Slovenia). He told us that the regime the Kosovo Albanians were subjected to could only be described as apartheid: their language was not recognized as an official language in Kosovo, they were denied schools in their language and a public cultural life. As a result, children were taught privately at home and alternative social institutions were established—and functioned very well in those times of crisis. By the late 1990s, as a result of Serbian politics and the involvement of the Yugoslav People's Army and Serbian paramilitary forces, the situation had escalated into one of the major national exoduses in Europe after World War II. Many Kosovars were killed or disappeared without a trace at that time.

In October 2000, I attended a conference on Balkan art in Thessaloniki as a member of Irwin. On October 5th, I joined other conference participants from all over former Yugoslavia in the hotel lobby. We were there to watch CNN's live coverage (dubbed in Greek) of the rally against Slobodan Milošević outside the Serbian Republican Assembly building in Belgrade. A part of the building was in flames, and although none of us understood Greek, we all knew that Milošević was irrevocably leaving the political arena, probably for good.

I happened to be sitting next to an artist from Kosovo, Sokol Beqiri, and we discussed the events in the then pan-Yugoslav lingua franca, Serbo-Croatian. He told me how, in 1999, he had had to vacate his house in a matter of minutes, and move his entire family from Peja to Montenegro. The old part of Peja was sacked and torched, its inhabitants displaced. The stories he told, about himself and his fellow townsmen, seemed like something from another era. But it had all happened then, and so very close to us. The Kosovars were only able to return to their homes in villages and towns after the NATO air raids and Milošević's capitulation. Sokol and I agreed: A military offensive was the only language Milošević understood and heeded. As Slavoj Žižek famously commented about the quandary whether to shell Belgrade or not: "My answer to the dilemma 'to bomb or not?' is: not enough bombs yet, and they are too late."

Sokol and I struck up a friendship, which led me to visit Kosovo a number of times. In 2002, working together with the artist Erzen Shkololli, Sokol organized the Irwin project *NSK Guard*, which entailed the Kosovan Army raising the flag of the NSK State in Time and guarding it for a while. I believe this was the time of the transformation of UÇK, the Kosovo Liberation Army, into the Army of the Republic of Kosovo. Before Sokol and Erzen could organize the project, they had to establish an NGO through which to communicate with public officials and the army; they called it Exit. In 2003, Sokol Beqiri, Mehmet Behluli, Shkelzen Maliqi, and Erzen Shkololli launched a pivotal project of the same name, EXIT, which involved developing and implementing an alternative educational program for the visual arts (theoretical and practical) with the financial support of the Berlin-based organization Relations. This was a great boost for the young Kosovan art scene and its contacts with the international art world. The old educational system was inadequate and riddled with problems, similar to the situation in most other successor states of former Yugoslavia. The alternative education program was launched because the artists-organizers were painfully aware of what was missing. As Sokol put it, he wanted to do something for the younger generations so they could fare better than he had; for instance, during his entire time at the Academy of Fine Arts in Prishtina, he never once heard artists like Joseph Beuys even mentioned. Thanks to EXIT, foreign curators, theorists, and gallerists started visiting Kosovo on a regular basis. A gallery was successfully opened in Peja. Kosovar artists started showing their work abroad. All in all, the EXIT project was a momentous initiative, but when the German funding ran out after a few very productive years, it unfortunately drew to a close. Nonetheless, the seed had been sown. It had been made clear to everyone that a local art scene cannot rely merely on artists participating in exhibitions abroad, and must develop its own art institutions and the basic elements of an art system.

Although Kosovo had virtually no functioning art system (and still does not have a satisfactory one), it has always abounded in incredible motivation and energy for good artistic production and for establishing art institutions and an art system. This was what swayed me to start going to Kosovo in 2003, mostly as an artist and sometimes privately or as a lecturer. I was enthused by people's desire to learn and high degree of self-organization, despite the inauspicious social circumstances and financial conditions. Also, in many other areas of life, I have witnessed great initiative on the part of the inhabitants of Prishtina, the town I am most familiar with in Kosovo, who have taken their fate into their own hands and try to survive by their own efforts. A part of the Kosovar art scene developed, and still maintains, the awareness that active engagement can accomplish a great deal in the long run, even when the conditions are dire.

The dichotomy between a new, very lively and good contemporary art production and the absence of the main elements of an art system, such as museums, galleries, art schools, art collectors, and theoreticians, is quite striking. Stepping up to partly fill this gap is Stacion – Center for Contemporary Art Prishtina, which I would like to present in more detail.

Faced with the institutional void, artist Albert Heta and architect Vala Osmani tackled the difficult task of forming a new institution, which required a great deal of self-organizing and hard work. Not least important was the choice of a name for an institution that in no way resembles an artist-run space and that can open or close without any serious consequences, depending on energy, motivation, and funds. Since the outset, Stacion has been staging exhibitions of both young local and prominent international artists.

Before founding Stacion, Albert Heta had attracted a lot of attention with two art projects: the opening of a Kosovo Embassy in Cetinje as part of the Cetinje Biennial in 2004, and the Kosovo Pavilion at the Venice Biennale in 2005, which only appeared as an advert in the online magazine *e-flux*. Heta explored the interspace between contemporary art, politics, and nationalism, a tendency contemporary art is not quite immune to anywhere in the world. (This subject was dealt with in a book edited and published in 2007 by Kosovan theoretician Sezgin Boynik and Finnish artist Minna Henriksson, *Contemporary Art and Nationalism: Critical Reader.*)

Stacion is a functional institution, making an important contribution to meeting the demands of the local contemporary art scene, despite its small size, and providing one of its key links with the international art scene. While obviously not sufficient for Kosovo, it is an important initiative that has sustained itself for more than ten years, a feat worthy of admiration. Stacion can also be seen as an art project, whose physical manifestation is a functional art institution.

Since 2015, Stacion has been organizing and producing its annual Summer School as School (SSAS), which fills a need by teaching contemporary art practices and theory in Kosovo and the wider region. It has been inspiring to watch the summer school develop into a consequential player for the region. In its first four years, it has hosted artists and theorists from the neighboring countries, the rest of Europe, and the United States. In my view, the SSAS has become Stacion's main project.

Understandably, the most relevant opinions about Stacion are those voiced by young artists, for whom Stacion has been of utmost importance throughout.

The artist Qëndresë Deda describes it thus:

> From my first contact with Stacion—in 2007, at the end of my high school years—I found interesting was what was happening there, which was different to the scene I knew by then. At Stacion, not only art was discussed but society, and social aspects as well. Beside exhibitions a deeper context to the works, and artists was provided. The exhibitions were accompanied with talks, which by then was new in Prishtina and thought-provoking for me. I had a chance to discuss art and my practice with the initiators of Stacion. This enabled me to receive broader knowledge and more support for my work. In my opinion, it was and still is an important place for artists and activists (especially for students now with SSAS), through creating a community discourse, providing space, spreading knowledge, and enabling us to build networks.

Building the underpinnings of an art system, without which no local art scene can function, Stacion is an emancipatory project and, as such, explicitly political, even without broaching topics related to daily politics.

The team of Stacion is aware that a cohesive collective is what makes for good projects, and for this reason they include younger generations in the production of exhibitions and projects.

According to the initiators of the project,

> Stacion – Center for Contemporary Art Prishtina is a project institution for contemporary art, design,

> and architecture. Established in 2006 by artist and designer Albert Heta and architect Vala Osmani, Stacion is a space for artists, architects, thinkers, designers, critics, and other sociopolitical workers committed to reflecting on and responding to relevant challenges in contemporary society with an active, critical, and emancipatory approach. Stacion – Center for Contemporary Art Prishtina functions as an open platform that employs strategies to build a dialogue with a differentiated public; works with clear social and political intents; encourages artistic practice and advanced architectural research, stands for intellectual independence; and works to create conditions where contemporary thought and practice can happen. Stacion is committed to the re-creation of the necessary momentum for the advancement and emancipation of the contemporary art scene and cultural environment of Kosovo. Stacion – Center for Contemporary Art Prishtina focuses on locally rooted practice as well as regional, European, and international processes.

I believe their words are justification enough for their work.

Working as an artist in a country with an undeveloped or poorly developed art system is a struggle due to the lack of institutional assistance; artists must often invest efforts into establishing an art system by themselves. The Irwin group had a similar experience in former Yugoslavia and later in the independent Slovenia, so I can understand the situation in Kosovo very well and am all in favor of projects like Stacion.

Another important site of change has been the National Gallery in Prishtina, especially since 2011, when artist Erzen Shkololli assumed the post of director. Under his leadership, the gallery blossomed into the central space for contemporary art in the wider region. Shkololli even managed to secure the support of the political top brass for the first national pavilion of Kosovo at the Venice Biennale in 2013, located in the Arsenale. Since then, Kosovar artists and architects have been appearing in Venice on a regular basis. And the National Gallery, now with Arta Agani at the helm, has been continuing to put on good exhibitions and in general maintaining the course set by its previous director.

As a guest in Kosovo, I have had the privilege of working together with people who do not work together amongst themselves as a rule. Art institutions and individual protagonists are usually like islands, hardly ever collaborating with one another. In my view, this is probably the weakest aspect of the otherwise burgeoning art scene, with a lot of room for improvement.

To sum up, I see Kosovo as a space that has evolved, thanks to outstanding artists and projects, from a nonexistent contemporary art scene to a substantial player in the regional and international arena. The protagonists of the Kosovo art system understand that they must collaborate with artists and art professionals from neighboring countries and in the region. This has led to Kosovo, and above all Prishtina, becoming a place where people from the former common country meet—for it is true, if we in the wider region do not organize ourselves, others will organize us.

WHAT COLOR IS YOUR FLAG WHEN IT BURNS?

A PERSONAL ACCOUNT OF NATIONALISM AND ART IN KOSOVO

Sezgin Boynik

One of the usual misunderstandings in thinking about the contemporary art practices of the Balkan countries is to approach them solely from the perspective of "the nation." This results in the dialectics between objective social conditions and the configurations of artistic subjectivities getting mediated and represented predominantly through the dynamics of nationalism. Accordingly, the shape that art takes is determined by the ideological forces maintained by a nation. In other words, the *kunstwollen* of an artwork, as Alois Riegl described it, is depicted through the shape that the nation gives to it. Riegl, an Austrian formalist art historian and one of the favorites of Walter Benjamin, described the dialectics of the production of artworks—in relation to contingencies of external social dynamics—through the process he called *kunstwollen*. This could be translated as "will to art," but more precisely it is about the constraints that the will, or intention, of the artist confronts during the process of artistic production. *Kunstwollen* alludes to a formal configuration as the artist carries out a primary negotiation or dialectical struggle with space-time and the material conditions of existence. It is the negotiation between the extrinsic outside ideology and the intrinsic formal rules of artistic figuration. How does this merging between outside and inside happen? In the case of nation and culture, as Carl Andre described very well in 1967, it occurs so that: "Art is what we do. Culture is what is done to us." In other words, the surroundings of the artist, the given ideological materials and elements—for example, language, history, and the cultural context as whole,—are always involved in the process of artistic production.

The usual problem with curatorial and representational attempts addressing the *kunstwollen* of Balkan artists is that they approach the understanding of their topic through the forces of the nation. This reduction of the dialectical relationship of art's intrinsic (formal) properties to one (usually national) determinant is similar to postcolonialist discussions surrounding the literature of the Third World nations. To those interested in the topic, I recommend the debate between Aijaz Ahmad and Fredric Jameson (both texts were published in the journal *Social Text* in 1987). Aijaz Ahmad criticized Jameson for interpreting Senegalese writer and filmmaker Ousmane Sembene's work through allegories that are consistently national. This, Ahmad notes, is symptomatic of leftist academic literary theory, which interprets the political dimension within the artistic production of Third World countries as projections of nationalism, thus simplifying complex constellations that contain other social determinants (especially those incorporating class struggles).

A cursory glance at international contemporary art exhibitions about Balkan art in the early 2000s shows this position in clear terms: René Block's exhibition *In the Gorges of the Balkans* was based on Karl May's kitschy fantasy about how the Balkan people embodied invariable national characteristics (Kunsthalle Fridericianum, Kassel, Germany, 2003); Harald Szeemann's exhibition *Blood and Honey: The Future's in the Balkans* (Essl Museum, Klosterneuburg, Austria, 2003), on the other hand, shared film director Emir Kusturica's vision of how people in the Balkan peninsula behave in good and bad times. These two exhibitions and several subsequent curatorial works—inside and outside of the Balkans—strengthen the position of "Balkanism," even in cases where the aim was to be critical of nationalist discourses in art practices. In 2006, as a reaction to this ongoing simplicity in regard to art made in Kosovo, Bosnia and Herzegovina, Serbia, Bulgaria, Albania, Romania, and other Balkan countries, we organized together with the Finnish artist Minna Henriksson—who shared an uneasiness about how René Block had exhibited artists from the Nordic counties through the lens of a certain predictable national/natural mystique—the conference Altered Identities at Stacion – Center for Contemporary Art Prishtina to address this problem complex. As a result of this intervention, we published following year a book titled *Contemporary Art and Nationalism: Critical Reader* (MM & EXIT Contemporary Art Center, Prishtina, 2007).

The theoretical background of the conference and the publication was based on the Louis Althusser's thesis on ideological interpellation. We claimed that, just as ideological state apparatuses draw subjects into ideology (i.e., subjectify them) through education, religion, media, etc., the institutions of contemporary art draw artists into the ideology of nationalism. We also claimed that this procedure of interpellation in contemporary art has a rigorous materialist existence, maintained through biennials, galleries, the managerial skills of curators, art critics, etc.; however, the procedure of interpellation has a more sophisticated characteristic. It incorporates into nationalist ideologies subjects who at the same time refuse to watch TV, listen to pop music, or cry at Hollywood movies. In the introduction to *Contemporary Art and*

Nationalism we claimed that this vicious operation is a dangerous one: it can appear progressive, while playing the regressive role of reproducing the national status quo. The book consists of three parts: the theoretical framing of these ideological operations; a chapter on the intrinsic nationalism of cultural policies of art; and finally, case studies dealing with various national(ist) art practices. My contribution was an examination of contemporary art in Kosovo and its relationship to nationalism.

The main argument of my text "Theories of Nationalism and Contemporary Art in Kosovo" (published in *Contemporary Art and Nationalism*) is that contemporary art made in Kosovo in the 2000s, despite its complexities and contradictory forms, was often seen only through the lenses of national ideologies. The artworks which had nothing to do with nationalism or questions regarding the nation were also interpreted in this way. Examples are Jakup Ferri's videos dealing with belatedness and the obscure creativity of being outside of art history, and Dren Maliqi's early installations and videos, which make absurdly beautiful and poetic statements about learning art history. Both have more in common with underground music or conceptual art than superficial questions of national identity. In 2003 and 2004, no young Kosovar contemporary artist in Prishtina—which Block praised as the center of the avant-garde in Europe—cared about nationalism. At that time, the question for these artists was how to orient their quest for formal innovations within institutions that were constraining them by all available means. There was no interest in policing the contemporary art world of Kosovo or networking in the global art world. The practical outcome of this was that no one was interested in curating the productive mess that was happening at that time in the art scene. The art was genuinely and instinctively outside of the state and its institutions.

My text, however, did not deal with the absence of nationalism in the works of Jakup Ferri or Dren Maliqi; instead, it addresses two artists, Albert Heta and Erzen Shkolloli, for whom national identity was seen as the primary focus of their art. The criticism I made departs from the thesis that a cultural policy preoccupied with national identity obviates some of the most important social and political questions faced in Kosovo: unemployment (reaching 60 percent), corruption among the comprador bourgeoisie, and the semi-colonial conditions of the state.

Today, looking back on this text, I would like to add some clarifications. First, the two artists who were the focus of my critique later on ceased to produce art and turned mostly to cultural policy, either as curators or managers of public and private institutions. I could say that their cultural trajectories proved my thesis on the direct relationship between cultural identity-based art practice and the national institutions.

I can, retrospectively, say that my thesis had a very absolutist idea of nationalism. At the time, in 2004, the question of nationalism had not yet reached its contradictory character of today, a result that followed the political intervention of the Vetëvendosje movement. In 2010, the Vetëvendosje movement—meaning "self-determination"—was reorganized as a party and continued its political struggle as an uneven formation. This unevenness of the organization, a mixture of a representative political party and a horizontal grassroots movement, is explicitly manifested in their articulation of the nation through a dialectics of struggle. This idea of nation could be described as a strange combination of Fanon and Lenin: the nation as an object that is never a complete and finished entity—as such, a nation (of people) can never serve to maintain the status quo. If the nation is something that constantly changes, consequently, the reclamation of nationalism makes sense only when it serves to politicize the masses in the process of dialectical voluntarism—as Peter Hallward describes it—outside of the state apparatuses. Once Vetëvendosje became the "voice" of opposition within the state apparatus—the Parliament— they faced the clear dead end of this contradiction. This sort of antagonistic nationalism within state institutions soon turned out to be incompatible with the normative rules of representational politics. Vetëvendosje, at this point, performed a radical leap, a certain political break, by not accepting the normative language of representational politics imposed on them by national state apparatuses. The outcome of this has been, since 2015, a continuous and determined intervention in parliamentary sessions, with the throwing of tear gas bombs inside the Kosovo Parliament. Apart from the question of violence, this radical act of interruption showed another thing: that nationalism is divided into two —the nationalism of the comprador bourgeoisie and the nationalism of the people are not the same. Whereas the former is only an instrument used by a few for the benefit of slicing up the public cake of the dependent nation-state, the latter is a nationalism of those who are excluded from the registers of culture and other state apparatuses. The second nationalism is genuinely against the normative state and the inequality it is imposing on the people. To put it in more familiar terms, Vetëvendosje, for a few years, has demonstrated that there is a difference between culturalist and organizational (or revolutionary) nationalism: one is about traditions while the other is concerned with shapes yet to come. They were defending a nation within a nation.

During 2004–06, this schism of nationalisms was barely visible; and in criticizing the nationalism of the artists, I failed to recognize that there could also be a possibility of a nation-formation staying consciously outside of the state apparatus. This is an important point to note, and I have made this long digression solely to underline the fact that a more experimental form of nationalism outside the state is possible: that the objective conditions of the state never allow for any other nationalism but the one that reaffirms itself through the language of the obvious and given realpolitik.

It is not only a nation that has, as a conjuncture, a strange relationship to art practices. The economy and politics can spoil the picture as well. Thus, the second argument of my thesis in the article written in 2006, on the nationalistic character of Kosovo contemporary art, has a similar conceptual error. By criticizing the content of artworks for not being concerned enough with the questions of a given economic situation, I have replaced one objective condition with another. Namely, the consideration of economic factors does not necessarily make art practices less ideological than a focus on the nationalist issue would. There is no guarantee that artworks dealing with economic inequalities do not reproduce the state-regulated understanding of the distribution of wealth. Simply, an artwork on unemployment can also be thought about in a way similar to the normative and ideological tendencies of the state.

Artistic subjectivity as something opposing the objectivity of the nation or state became explicitly visible when, in 2008, a group of curators tried to open an exhibition of contemporary artists from Kosovo in Belgrade, Serbia. The exhibition, entitled *Exception: Contemporary Art Scene from Prishtina*, was organized by two NGOs (Kontekst from Belgrade and Napon from Novi Sad, Serbia) and was curated by Kristian Lukić, Gordana Nikolić, Ivana Marjanović, and Vida Knežević. The exhibition, as planned, was first opened on January 22, 2008, at the Museum of Contemporary Art of Vojvodina, Novi Sad, by the President of the Assembly of the Autonomous Province Vojvodina, Bojan Kostreš. However, the scheduled opening of the same exhibition at the Kontekst Gallery in Belgrade on February 7, 2008, was violently interrupted by the demonstration of the neo-Nazi group Obraz, and also a painter who declared himself an academic and a member of ULUS (the Association of Fine Artists of Serbia), and an anonymous person who vandalized Dren Maliqi's work *Face to Face* (2003), which consisted of pop icon Elvis Presley and Kosovo Liberation Army fighter Adem Jashari facing each other with guns in a duel. The police forces that were present to secure the exhibition opening decided that it was not safe to go ahead with the ceremony. Consequently, *Exception* was cancelled. Considering that Kosovo was preparing to declare its independence at the time of the planned exhibition opening, and that a presidential election was expected to be held in Serbia, this was not a suitable cultural event in Serbian political life. This exceptional event mobilized almost all artists, theoreticians, activists, art historians, and curators of the Serbian artistic scene.

The incident led to the formation of a collective directly dealing with political issues related to the closure of the exhibition, and many journals and magazines gave a considerable amount of attention to this event.

This was neither the first nor last occasion for contemporary artists of Kosovo to exhibit in Belgrade after 1999. In 2006, Lulzim Zeqiri, Alban Muja, and Driton Hajredini presented their work at the Kontekst Gallery, and Jakup Ferri exhibited his work at the 47th October Salon. In 2008, Nurhan Qenaja and Fitore Isufi / Koja exhibited at the 49th October Salon. All of these events were organized by the Cultural Centre of Belgrade, which was founded by the City of Belgrade. However, the timing of *Exception* was very exceptional. This was a clear reminder that artistic subjectivities have a very complex and contradictory relationship with national and state objectivities. In the text I wrote about the incident ("Theory of Incident: How to Think the Relationship of Art and Politics beyond Functionalism – The Case of Closure of the Exception: Contemporary Art Scene from Prishtina Exhibition in Belgrade, 7th February 2008," published in 2013), I analyzed this contradictory situation by looking at the theoretical and critical studies related to this event. The first thing to notice about the exhibition is that it became a sort of radiograph of Serbian-Albanian relations from the perspective of art. In this incident, the components of the contradictory relationship between nationalism and art became evident. Even though the curators of the exhibition did everything to avoid an ethnic representation of Kosovar artists—as the title of the show didn't mention Albanian artists, but artists from Prishtina instead—still, the concept of the exhibition was centered on the question of identity. The whole issue revolved around the way the curators from Serbia represented the artists from Kosovo. The most apparent thing to notice, on the formal level, was the way curators conceived the role of art in society. In the introduction to the exhibition catalogue, they situated their task within the fields of "communication" and "coexistence," which might be manifested through art. In fact, the curators' general conception of "art" itself was functionalist. As they define it, "the field of art is a place where, among other things, people talk about something that has to be talked about publicly, in the media and the Parliament; the issue of the past, the issue of the future of coexistence in this region, and the issue of the very subject." This functionalism (or objectifying of art practice) easily adapted itself to the democratic functionalism regarding the representation of national minorities inside the state apparatus.

Yet, there was another strong position in interpreting the incident, put forward by Branimir Stojanović, a psychoanalyst based in Belgrade, who refused to understand the situation using normative language. He insisted on seeing the emptiness of the exhibition space as similar to the void of the non-representable nature of the state in its totality; or, precisely, to associate the emptiness of the exhibition—that didn't take place—with the void of disturbing elements not indexed in the catalogue of the state. In the case of the Serbian state, these elements are, of course, Albanians—elements structurally opposite to everything that keeps the Serbian state apparatus together. Stojanović, by underlining this non-representability of Albanians, showed that breaking away from the normative language of the state can be made to happen by passing through these voids. The thoughts and subjectivities of arts (as well as politics) have to belong to this realm.

If Albanians are one such void, and a disturbing factor for the state, then any other factor or event that has a similar characteristic has to be included within the theory. The closure of the *Exception* exhibition is one such case; it enables analysis of the incident to seek the subjectivity and the singularity of thought beyond objective conditions. According to Stojanović, contemporary art is another such disturbing factor in the eyes of the administrative state apparatus of Serbia. On a different occasion, Stojanović claimed that the Kosovar art scene would cease to be as interesting and productive as it is, as the country gained its independence. More or less, this is what happened: indeed, the art produced after Kosovo's independence is less interesting than before.

However, the reason for this is not that art produced under the sovereign state loses its autonomy; the real cause is the strange relationship between state and art. By contrast, the conditions of a weak or nonexistent state provide artistic and political subjectivities that are richer and more contradictory. The same happened with the art exhibitions that addressed the perplexing question of the relationship between states—for example, between Kosovo and Serbia. Most exhibitions dealing with relationships like this are coordinated through organizations and institutions that are not directly linked to the state. For example, the exhibition *Exception* was organized by two NGOs, as most of the cultural events dealing with Kosovo in Belgrade were housed by an NGO called CzKD (Center for Cultural Decontamination). Of course, there is always the question whether these NGOs really are independent from the state; but at least they provoked interesting theoretical discussions on the nature of the state, nationalism, economy, and other objective given conditions.

Following on from these remarks, it is today interesting to examine the ideological conditions of exhibitions bringing together artists from Kosovo and Albania (*The Whale That Was A Submarine. Contemporary Positions from Albania and Kosovo*, Ludwig Museum, Budapest, 2016). Since the ethnic tensions cannot be a point of departure in thinking about the relationship between these two sovereign states, it is important to see how curators and artists are seeing this amalgamation. Thus, the exhibition dealing with an Albania-Kosovo connection, the first to my knowledge, can play an interesting role by pointing out—even if unwittingly—the role of state strictures in artistic configurations. One thing is clear: Albania didn't play any important role in the formation and development of the contemporary art scene in Kosovo. It was socialist Yugoslavia, and especially the conflicts, antagonisms, and conditions of post-Yugoslav states, that were crucial to the formation of artists from Kosovo. The relationship with Albania is a recent development. In 2016, while this exhibition in Budapest was under preparation, the Kosovo artist Alban Muja, who was given Albanian honorary citizenship, had an exhibition in the gallery of COD – Center for Openness and Dialogue in Tirana. Conceived and opened by the Albanian Prime Minister, Edi Rama, the exhibition was organized in the building housing the prime minister's office. However, Shkelzen Maliqi, who curated several contemporary art shows and worked on the non-governmental cultural and artistic relationships between Kosovo and other post-Yugoslav states, was adviser to Edi Rama concerning the "Balkan question" during 2016.

The relationship between Albanian and Kosovar art exists today mostly on the state and administrative level, so it will be interesting to see how artistic subjectivities will confront these objective circumstances.

2018 Afterword

This text was commissioned for the catalogue of the exhibition *The Whale That Was A Submarine. Contemporary Positions from Albania and Kosovo,* Ludwig Museum, Budapest, 2016, curated by Jula Fabényi and Borbála Kálmán. My idea was to discuss how uninteresting, unproductive, and futile it was to question art forms and inquiries through the lenses of nationalism. Now, in the political conjuncture of 2018, arguments in the text need some further clarifications.

From the beginning of 2018, Vetëvendosje has gone through a huge change. Some members inclined to solidify the parliamentary party structures inside the movement have split from Vetëvendosje, calling themselves the Social Democratic Party of Kosovo. While splinters play the usual political game, the core of the Vetëvendosje movement is now calling for clarifications of the national question within their political mandate, which is self-determination and dialectical voluntarism. The political conjuncture is now pressing the cultural nationalists to declare their position regarding the state apparatuses even more clearly and boldly. For contemporary art today, operating inside the structures of culture, the most demanding question is about not the nation but the state.

During this political confusion, an artist from Prishtina, Driton Selmani, has replaced the Albanian national flag with the football offside flag as an artistic intervention commenting on the confusion of national representation. After a few hours, he was interrogated by the police and was almost lynched by the media.

Selmani says that "only after doing the intervention did he understand how attached nationalism is to our skin." Here is the question this intervention calls for: What are the invisible sources of incessant nationalism if not the same as the structures that are reproducing the semi-comprador bourgeoisie operating secretly inside the state?

MOM AND DAD ARE FRIGHTENED THAT WE WILL END UP LIKE DON QUIXOTE

TETRIS: PRISHTINA POST WASHINGTON COAST

Alush Gashi

It was never going to be easy, putting in place the few bolts holding that old house together at St. Mark Isaku in downtown Prishtina. Some said it might crumble down before the guys put up a show—or played the first few riffs. The neighbors were anxious and properly puzzled: who are the dudes bringing in all those vintage keyboards and "monuments," as they called art pieces and antiques?

The house owner—or Bami, as he was nicknamed colloquially—was a bit skeptical about the whole operation, but he was like "Fuck it, I'll let them do their thing and collect my rent on time." He and his brother owned most of the neighborhood, or at least so Bami claimed. They were tough guys with nothing to lose and post-1999 Kosovo suited their style perfectly. They were in the business of renting properties to shady people and artists alike, no questions asked and no contracts signed, and business was booming. They weren't paying taxes or electricity bills. The electricity bill collector showed up once, but Bami shredded the invoice to pieces and blew it into collector's face. Needless to say, the meter never stopped running.

On September 19, 2009, Tetris was ready. They called it a "manipulation space," for lack of a less manipulative term. Nobody had anything close to a preconceived idea of what to do on Day One of operations. The crowds from Tingle Tangle, the arty bar that Tetris's founders were also running at another location in Prishtina, would surely be interested in checking out the new space and giving their five cents on the crushingly pale white color dominating the interior and the state of the toilets—or perhaps throw around an idea or two about the programming, if there was ever going to be such a thing. But the people were curious and expectant; they wanted to participate, be included; the more ambitious wanted to take over the proceedings.

Initially, people treated Tetris with caution, voyeurism, and platonic lust. It was an artist-run space with charisma and potential, crammed in an environment that could potentially give young artists what they needed: freedom and a voice. True, there were exhibition spaces around Prishtina at that time, but those came with curators and questionnaires. Kids in those days didn't need a sense of direction, they needed an option to get lost. Tetris was the perfect platform for creating an imaginary world, free of standards and prejudices, in a decade-after-the-war Kosovo that had reality bites all over its torn body. The young and the bold embraced that fact and threw in a collective burst of ideas: they were embraced back by Tetris, and the space's identity began to take shape.

In the five years Tetris officially operated as a public venue, it hosted more than fifty events—including art exhibitions, film screenings, theater performances, workshops, talks, and concerts. Some of the first artists to emerge from Kosovo's postwar cultural scene examined a societal approach to art through the *Perspektiva* exhibition in June 2010, curated by Erzen Shkololli. Jakup Ferri, Rron Qena, Agim Balaj, Jeton Gusia, and other Kosovo-born-and-raised artists in their mid-to-late twenties also manipulated Tetris to suit personal twists in their homeland's fairytale. Even the Handsome Furs, the Montreal-based indie rock duo led by Dan Boeckner of

Wolf Parade, had a gig co-organized by Tetris in August 2011. But it was the collective spirit of participatory intrusions that would distinguish Tetris from other similar ventures. The interventionists couldn't get enough of this oddball space that gave meaning to their artistic existence; they just wanted to mingle, and mingle they did.

Tetris was a project that united Kosovo's art scene around a cohesive concept of "creative solidarity." Despite some of the egos charged by the space being "the size of Texas" (to paraphrase Bill Callahan slightly), they were immediately shrunk when faced with the solidarity of the artistic community, which opted for a joint output during interventions. It was as if contrasting schools of thought decided to defy their respective contradictions and succumb to the collectivity. This wasn't a conformist approach at all; it actually radicalized the thinking process and turned it into a rather complicated quest for a unique and all-encompassing achievement. Take Angry Youth's collective manipulation of Tetris during the REDO Design Conference's third edition in November 2013. The exhibiting artists depicted glimpses of Prishtina's cheerful cityscape, absorbed the critique implying that it lacked grim impressions, and then decided to turn Tetris into a dark city covered in Caligari-esque pictorials. The resulting compromise was a void of imperfections and inadequacies, perfectly illustrating Angry Youth's innocence and latent charm.

Tetris Band was probably the main direct (documented) output that came out of the inner creative process that happened on the premises. With the help of slam poetry and delta blues echoing down the lonely streets of a river-less city, the Tetris in-house band brought art outfitters into the realm of creating music.

These soundscapes were based on hypnotic phrases from a myriad of synths and deep bass. The band's ever-changing line-up was prone to heavy analogue manipulation of screeching guitars, classical piano, and monotonous beats, adding color to their unpredictable yet explosive performances. Most of the participating musicians had limited musical training, relying solely upon rhythmic (dis)harmonies. In addition, an interest in obscure synths from the DIY era gave them the expansiveness their creativity required: the phrases were raw, the sound was ruthless, and the lyrics were non-negotiable. Hundreds, if not thousands, of hours of session recordings have piled up for years, waiting to be explored and released. To this day, Tetris, its music and its legacy go beyond the Tetris space and transcend into the territory of unexplored nostalgia, yearning for recognition.

In May 2014, Tetris decided to close its doors for the general public and remain a space to be used only by the members of the collective. After five intensive years, the crew felt it was time for reflection and self-evaluation. The revolution-hungry kids were becoming hungrier by the day; it was time to relinquish them so they could find another deviant spell.

This period of assumed calmness produced some of the collective's most memorable artworks. Alban Nuhiu's dark, brutalist photographs from that period showcased vibrant and intriguing transactions between hope and suspense. Nuhiu's film and video works were packed with unassuming portrayals of colorful characters that communicated multiple layers of emotions through the disciplined dynamics of his lens.

The subliminal connotations in Vigan Nimani's paintings and drawings were usually exposed when confronted with the uncertain realities from which they (tried to) emerge. The fading world he depicted from these years was full of such elegant uncertainties, making the cohabitation struggle between open spaces, buildings, nature, and humans even more evident. Then again, the architecture in his work felt empty without the natural interventions, sometimes as subtle as a tree shadow gracing a plain facade; human lives were telling stories of escape, isolation, and despair, in constant search for a cure to existential anxieties. Eventually, however, they all became properties in the interplay of emotions that shaped Nimani's impalpable world, full of longing and hope.

Bami was not getting enough money action and he decided that, after seven years, Tetris had to leave their original space. Hey, it was an economically dismal 2016 and a call center had made an offer on the premises that a shrewd businessman like Bami could not refuse. He offered Tetris a tiny house just down the block that some time ago had accommodated another art space called Te Dudi; the place had been abandoned for more than two years and was being used as an improvised dog shelter. Being confined within the tight space of these new four walls resulted in an interesting (group) transition for the members of the collective, who were now focusing solely on their music and existential discomforts. Rock 'n' roll was still there, but so were creative rifts and strong personalities.

Bami was worried: is the band gonna make it?

Just as Tetris decided they had enough of the neighborhood's gloomy outlook and began packing their synths, there was a sudden twist of fate. In April 2018, Tetris was comfortably relocated to a socialist-era building in downtown Prishtina that houses a 300-seat cinema and a concert stage the size of, well, Kansas. The cinema had been closed in 1988 by the Yugoslav military that occupied the space at that time, and was then used privately by the international administration in Kosovo (the United Nations and European Union Rule of Law Mission) since 1999. Thirty years after the initial shutdown, ARMATA, as it is now called, reopened as a public space promoting alternative culture and social dialogue. ARMATA had just begun an identity quest and was contemplating the idea of developing a longer-term publicly-infused program. Tetris was all about the infusion, and its synths got a new home. At the time of writing, their major concern was whether the Roland Juno-60 synth will sound the same on the new mixing console they're about to purchase; the shift from analogue to digital is making everyone at Tetris really nervous.

All that is left from the building where Tetris originated is a fence and the graffiti "Prishtina Post Washington Coast." Bami, the business trendsetter, decided that parking lots were the future and tore the whole neighborhood down. What he could not erase from the grounds was that awkward, lingering smell of curiosity and manipulation.

The band made it.

AUTHOR'S NOTE:

Tetris was founded by Vigan Nimani, Alban Nuhiu, and Jeton Rushiti. Besides its founders, the Tetris collective has also included Jakup Ferri, Burim Gora, Adem Hasani, Edmond Krasniqi-Eka, Arif Muharremi, and Bujar Sylejmani.

MELTING LEAD UNDER THE MOON, FOR THE SPRING BLOOMING SOON

INSTITUTING AND NETWORKING

Charles Esche

When Erzen Shkololli took over the directorship of the National Gallery of Kosovo, he took on an institution with an important history but an undefined future. Like much in Kosovo after the war, the situation was ripe with possibility, but the museum needed to be given a new sense of mission and purpose. The core question was whether the National Gallery would focus only on its national agenda and responsibilities, or whether it would also seek to build alliances beyond the borders of the new state. The tension between these two directions is one shared by almost all modern and contemporary art institutions, if not all cultural institutions in general. Modern art is both a product and symbol of unique national characteristics, and a language that connects promiscuously with international movements and non-national groups aligned by gender, ethnicity, or politics. Thus, Jackson Pollock can be both the quintessential US artist and his paintings can be symbols of international, even universal, masculine abstraction; Ai Wei Wei is both a Chinese dissident and a nomadic artist working within the global contemporary tradition of installation and performance art; Louise Bourgeois is a product of sophisticated French patriarchy and a key artist of international feminism; and so on. Each aspect of the artists' specific or universalist attributes can be emphasized depending on the story a curator or museum director wants to tell. For Shkololli, the first question was how to orient the National Gallery of Kosovo in this contested art dynamic, and how to inspire an emerging

Kosovar art scene in a way that it would not lose its specificity—nor endanger the tender shoots of national cultural revival by overwhelming it with international competition. Given the new director's history, his choice to seek out the European and international art world might seem a given. Yet his institutional answer was a more nuanced step to use the National Gallery as a bridge between the "here" of Prishtina and Kosovo and the "there" of the international art world, and as a route by which Kosovar artists could gain international recognition and opportunities while remaining connected to their origins.

To understand what Shkololli brought to the job, it is important to know that he began his career as an artist and will one day, I hope and suspect, return to making his own artworks. Indeed, it was while I was installing an exhibition of his work in CAPC Bordeaux, with the Israeli curator Galit Eilat, that he told me about his appointment as director of the National Gallery. So while we curators were discussing with him the embroideries he made during the Kosovo War, he began to discuss with us what it would mean to run the National Gallery and how he would approach the job.[1] I have to admit to some surprise when he announced his new position. He was increasingly visible in the art world and had been already selected for a number of international exhibitions and collections. To become a museum director necessarily meant turning his back on that career, at least for a time, and committing to a different kind of life in which his activities would be in the service of other artists and the cultural community in Kosovo in general. It was impressive to see the passion with which he embraced this change.

From the very beginning of his tenure, it was clear that Shkololli would act quickly on his vision and forge a new series of connections between the National Gallery of Kosovo and the international art world. He immediately invited René Block, the legendary German curator who was already engaged with the Balkan art scene, and asked him to prepare an exhibition. It was for similar reasons that I first came to Kosovo. I was invited, again with Galit Eilat, to curate the 2012 edition of the Muslim Mulliqi Prize. Together with the Gjon Mili Photography Prize, this exhibition is historically a platform that gives emerging artists and photographers in Kosovo an opportunity to introduce themselves and their work to a wider public. Shkololli set out to maintain traditions inherited from the valuable work of his predecessors, while injecting new energy and ambition into the works' presentation. He shifted both exhibitions to a biannual basis, ensuring he could offer support for new artistic production and more resources could be put into each edition. He also chose to reduce the huge number of relatively simple exhibitions held at the National Gallery each year, opting for longer shows. This created time and a little financing to develop the exhibitions, as well as initiate an educational and public lecture program. In this way, a number of international art figures—including Adam Szymczyk, Kathrin Rhomberg, and Hans-Ulrich Obrist—as well as artists and others from Kosovo, could deliver lectures for the artistically interested public and university students in Prishtina. In turn, visiting international curators were able to see works made in Kosovo and potentially invite their makers for exhibitions or projects elsewhere.

Of course, Shkololli's efforts to reschedule and redraw the National Gallery of Kosovo's program were intended to have an impact on the level of public interest in the institution, but more fundamental to his approach was a new way of thinking about the institution in terms of its presence in the art scene, both locally and internationally. What he did could be understood as an institutionalization of the National Gallery, in which he redefined its purpose and mission for conditions in a new state. This does not mean constructing a completely new museum, and the new director took particular care to refresh some of the basic programs that he had inherited from the past, such as the two major prize exhibitions. This whole process must also be seen against the background of mistrust in institutions inherent to the recent history of Kosovo. Shkololli was therefore attempting to both establish the idea of a "national gallery," as well as define what roles his specific institution in Prishtina should be performing and what it should leave to other actors. As he said in an interview towards end of his tenure: "I think we are all obliged as citizens of Kosovo, which is a very young country, to make a contribution—I really wanted, and I still want, to contribute to my country, at least with what I think I know the best." The crucial element in this sentence is this idea of "knowing best," as it points to how he could mobilize his network and his skills in the service of the National Gallery. In practical terms, what this commitment meant was to try to shape the National Gallery of Kosovo around a new set of institutional priorities. While he brought in his specific personal network, which was only going to be available to the National Gallery during his directorship, he also implemented goals that would endure beyond his tenure, As we have seen, he put more resources into fewer exhibitions and started an educational and lecture program. These were structural improvements that allowed a more sustainable institution to emerge. Within the public sphere in the city, his changes also shifted the identity of the building. It became less a simple showroom for art, in which the university's art teachers and a wider group of artists would have rotating opportunities to show the latest work from their studios on its walls. Instead, the exhibitions became scarcer and more structured, with group and solo exhibitions backed by curatorial research. Gradually, it became a place where debates about the nature of contemporary art and its role in Kosovo's internationalization, as well as the nature of the country's cultural specificity, could take place.

On a personal basis, I still well remember the discussions that took place around the 2012 Muslim Mulliqi prize—with Shkololli, gallery assistants Nita Deda and Rina Meta, and graphic designer Bardhi Haliti—about artists in Kosovo. They introduced me to the longer history of the region and how it impacted art practices today, thus allowing me to understand the work we selected for the exhibition much more clearly. The exhibition was based in part on open submissions, and going through the submitted slides gave us a good overview of what was happening in the country, something we could then back up with research visits to different cities. Thus, the National Gallery served not only to introduce two international curators to Kosovo art but also to allow us to talk to and exchange our experience directly with artists for whom traveling was not always so easy. As a result, Galit Eilat and I were able to include some non-Kosovar artists as well as a couple of works from the Van Abbemuseum's collection that seemed relevant to us on the basis of what we had seen and heard. Even the title *It doesn't have to be beautiful, unless it's beautiful* was intended to point up the tension between a public desire for art to be beautiful and a more metropolitan aspiration for art to be critique. I was therefore happy when our efforts to understand the complexity of Kosovo and the relation between the city and the land was in some way rewarded with the choice, by a jury that included Zdenka Badovinac and Vasif Kortun, of rurally based Fatos Kabashi, for his pencil lead sculptures. Kabashi's work, a perfect marriage of craft skill and a strong, slightly crazy concept, captured the meaning of the exhibition title. I greatly valued the dialogues I had with people around the institution, and these were hopefully reflected back in the exhibition itself, with works from Mehmet Behluli, Shpend Havolli, and Majilinda Hoxha particularly standing out. I was only one of a number of people who benefitted from this approach, and many went on to include Kosovar artists in their international projects, most notably documenta 14 in 2017.

This new vision of the National Gallery of Kosovo was not confined to major group exhibitions, such as the Mulliqi and Mili prizes, but also extended to properly researched solo exhibitions with catalogues, featuring some of the most significant Kosovar artists—such as Sokol Beqiri, Lala Meredith-Vula, and Muslim Mulliqi. Having established a clear direction for the National Gallery that was both more academic in terms of art history, and more discursive in terms of public interaction, Shkololli's next step was to move beyond the walls and to further internationalize Kosovo's cultural presence by advocating for a Kosovo Pavilion at the Venice Biennale. His political efforts succeeded in 2013 with Petrit Halilaj's very well-received contribution, curated by Kathrin Rhomberg, with Shkololli serving as commissioner of the Kosovo Pavilion. Since then, Flaka Haliti (2015) and Sislej Xhafa (2017) have appeared in Venice and Kosovo is now also part of the Architecture Biennale in Venice. All of these steps not only promote the artists themselves—which has to be part of the museum's brief in a city without a strong commercial art scene—but also energized the field of art history writing in Kosovo, launching the construction of a narrative of 21st-century contemporary artistic development in the country. This new narrative, and the inevitable disputes around it, can in turn serve as a clearer source of inspiration and argument for current and future artistic generations.

There are, however, two areas to which Shkololli paid less attention and which need to be addressed in any assessment of his time in charge of the National Gallery of Kosovo. One concerns the National Gallery's collection of artworks, how they are stored, and how the insitution animates them in its exhibitions. By focusing on supporting new work and intelligently curating retrospectives of older Kosovar artists, Shkololli was probably too stretched to deal properly with the National Gallery's important historic art collection. This lack perhaps points to a weakness in his methodology of institutional renewal, though one that can still be corrected. A museum's collection is always its core material; to work outwards from the collection allows a museum to develop a longer-term legacy and a more secure right to exist when competing for scarce cultural resources. By not placing the collection centrally, Shkololli's program, arguably, was too invested in representing his network and his generation of artists, and neglected a longer or more antagonistic history of different movements and tendencies within the history of Kosovar art. As a result, the National Gallery of Kosovo could potentially find itself in a more precarious or antagonistic political position than if it used the collection to tell a national cultural story across generations. While this story can still be formulated through future artistic visions of the National Gallery, it remains a missed opportunity, although an understandable one given that so much had to be squeezed into a directorship of only four years.

Second, his attempts to influence the state of the Academy of Fine Arts in Prishtina, and therefore of the teaching of new Kosovar artists, largely failed, but this was much less in Shkololli's control. As in many smaller art ecologies, a lot is dependent on a flow of young talent from art courses in order to renew the discourse and experiment with different forms of making art. By setting a new benchmark for national artists in his exhibitions and research, it was to be hoped that the traditions of academic art teaching would respond and attempt to renew themselves. Unfortunately, there is as yet little sign of this happening. On the positive side, it is good to see independent institutions, such as Stacion and the commercial gallery LambdaLambdaLambda, flourishing in Prishtina after Shkololli's departure.

One final question mark that has, by some, been placed over Shkololli's directorship is the political nature of the work he supported. Given the recent history of the country, some expected a more politicized artistic program—but in my opinion that is to misunderstand the nature of a "national art gallery." A national gallery must follow artistic developments on the ground while innovating and developing its institutional infrastructure. It is up to the independent sector instead to generate alternatives and new political positions within the arts that can subsequently push the National Gallery to incorporate them into its own programs. Art exists in an ecology of artists, writers about art, and various institutions, and the

National Gallery is as dependent on independent initiatives as they are on it.

What is beyond dispute is that Erzen Shkololli has left a substantial legacy of institutional invention and a promising ground on which to build. The question for the next decade of Kosovar art is to what extent that promise and potential can be fulfilled.

1 The exhibition was called *Strange and Close* and featured works from the Van Abbemuseum collection at CAPC Bordeaux. It was curated by Galit Eilat and myself, together with colleagues from the Van Abbemuseum, Eindhoven.

TRADITIONALLY UNCOMFORTABLE

IT IS AS IT IS NOT SLEEPING, IT FLOATS LIKE A SPACESHIP

Kathrin Rhomberg

A strange structure has invaded the 55th Venice Biennale and squeezed itself into the white cube of the Kosovo Pavilion. Representing Kosovo in its first-ever national pavilion, Petrit Halilaj has created a massive hovering structure, built—or rather, woven—out of dead branches, twigs, and mud. Taking up almost two-thirds of the space, the object strikes us as an alien sight, atavistic within the Biennale's context of contemporary art; a foreign body which has migrated from some subconscious territory or forgotten era into the most iconic exhibition of the historic Western world's cultural and artistic achievements. As if the ground were not to be entirely trusted, the structure hovers—like the landing-apparatus of some fictitious spacecraft—slightly above the gallery's floor, on dainty iron supports that take the peculiar form of oversized bird's feet. The object's detachment from the ground adds a certain ambiguity to its appearance, recalling vague images of a bird's nest or a primordial shelter, as well as those of some kind of utopian spacecraft. But the object invites our investigation: there is an opening in its side, encouraging those adventurous enough to enter into its interior. Once inside, the musty, earthy smell intensifies and the materiality of the dead branches and twigs becomes far more physically tangible. Following a narrow passageway, a small hole in the branches and twigs is revealed, offering a peek into another interior space. The brightly shining white walls of this inner space stand in sharp contrast to the darkness of the passageway; a contrast so striking that it lends the room the qualities of a totally separated inner world, or some kind of "mental space." Its walls are not angular, but rounded—their shape echoing the curves of the object's outer walls.

At first sight, the only feature this bare interior space hosts is the extended reach of the structure's wild, pervasive branches into a strangely protruding ceiling. One can also see, hooked to the lower branches, several dispersed clothes hangers. From one of the furthest reaching, a bright canary-yellow costume is hung. Without being able to detect any obvious explanation for the presence of the clothing or the clothes hangers, one cannot help but perceive a certain absence in the room. Who does the dress belong to? Who made it, and why? Given the particular nature of the surrounding structure, and the ambiguity provoked by clothes hanging inside an otherwise unoccupied room, the setting elicits a surreal sensation: one is confronted by the presence of an absent owner. Someone is not present, or is no longer there; has not yet returned, or has simply not yet arrived. Nothing seems final or permanent, nothing definite. Above all else it is this kind of intermediate state that specifies the interior room as a space of possibilities and potentialities, a situation in transition. This is intensified by the experience of being covered with the darkness of the passageway, which is a kind of Benjaminian hybrid—a form that occupies the space between exterior and interior.[1]

This inner white room is, however, not entirely unoccupied. There are two canaries fluttering about and chirping, leaving their traces on the white floor. But their presence further emphasizes the feeling of an absence. Since the birds must assume a dependency on a human keeper (canaries being otherwise unfit to survive naturally in these parts of the world), one cannot but wonder who, or where, this owner might be. Keeping birds also somehow characterizes a person: perhaps they appear as stand-ins for something missing, for unspoken longings and unfulfilled hopes.

Given the dark, stifling tightness of the structure's passageway through which one has squeezed, the canaries bring another association to mind: their sentinel role in the coal mines of the past to warn of imminent danger. So as long as they are fluttering about, chirping happily, or just perching somewhere, then everything is fine, whatever the potential hazards of the surroundings might be.

Petrit Halilaj's works are often rooted in the necessity to search for what the essence of reality might be, through a presence torn between a distorted past and an uncertain future. His project at the Venice Biennale seems to have blended the experiences of his transnational way of life —a life of moving between Kosovo (where he grew up and where his family and many friends live), Italy (where he studied and where his foster parents live), and Berlin (where he is currently living). It is a permanently transitory and unstable existence. In much the same way as his other previous projects, Halilaj initiated an open process of joint reflection in which his family and others close to him were actively involved. He claims it was his mother's suggestion to develop a sheltered structure within a structure—an idea not all unlike any family within any society—to allow him to develop his ideas, free from any assumed expectations and the pressures of representing such a young nation celebrating its first appearance at the Venice Biennale. Halilaj has confronted these assumed expectations by displaying personal materials and contents, connected only with him. The two canaries, housed in the exhibition for its entire duration, were moved from his studio and home in Berlin, which he shares with his partner. The yellow costume hanging in the interior space was made to the size of his body by female Kosovar tailors who are colleagues of his mother. The clothes hangers were made by his grandfather for his new home, to welcome the dresses of his "future wife." The branches, twigs, and even the earth were all collected from Runik, the area in Kosovo where he grew up.

The poetic setting of these interwoven materials and contents, which appears at first to create a purely protective space, proves to be the setting of a sensitive transition—a space within a space where Halilaj's different worlds and realities can come together and any divisions between art and nature, subject and object, reality and imagination, can be set aside.

The structure not only evokes a space of shelter for humans and birds, but also one of possibilities and potentialities that enables a longing for future schemes, perspectives, and prospects to unfold—an almost utopian desire that may also speak of the shared experience that preceded his project in Venice.

Through its continuous attempts to translate the "one" into the "other," this project exemplifies Halilaj's specific way of exploring art and reality. But despite its obvious personal and intimate nature, it clearly carries a wider and more general representation of reality, one that is ceaselessly affected by the experiences of alienation incited by the radical sociopolitical and economical shifts of today's world. Not least, it also carries hope for Kosovo, a nation still in the making, and still struggling two decades after the war that formed it. Nothing seems to be final or definite.

We are searching for a way to shape our nation. And sometimes we have too great an urge to find out who we are. The yellow dress does not define who you are. Maybe it abstracts who you are even further. And in doing so it opens up spaces of possibilities, and maybe even utopian moments. But how weird it is to call them utopian... Not because they are utopian things—they are so real. But utopian in the sense that they are impossible to be shared in the way that we need them. Sharing means to live them and to move further. It is the same with the pavilion. The moment you enter it you are part of it, sharing the intimacy with the birds and the objects. The birds are watching you and you are watching them. But the structure is fragile. It is not sleeping, it floats like a spaceship.

(Petrit Halilaj)

First published in Petrit Halilaj, *I'm hungry to keep you close. I want to find the words to resist but in the end there is a locked sphere. The funny thing is that you're not here, nothing is*, Venice Biennale, Verlag der Buchhandlung Walther König, 2014.

1 Walter Benjamin, *The Arcades Project*, Harvard University Press, Cambridge, MA 2002, p. 422.

BABY BLUES

SPECULATING ON THE BLUE

Vanessa Joan Müller

The horizon commonly describes a demarcation line, both in a spatial and temporal sense, for that which is not yet within reach, for that which, perhaps, cannot even be imagined yet or has been classified as simply impossible by the dominant order. Despite its utopian potential, the horizon as the delineation of a border, even in its figurative sense, cannot be separated from its position within the here and now. It sketches questions and answers that we deem meaningful from a certain perspective within this horizon, but we are unable to introduce into our scope the very horizon that helps to shape it. It is therefore also a metaphor for something which lies constantly before our eyes, which is indispensable for our perspective, but which ultimately can never be reached.

From an ideological standpoint, the horizon has long designated an idea of the future: a better tomorrow in terms of movement and progress. Today, the idea of the horizon is often tied to the notion of a threshold – of that which can only be imagined but never experienced. The historian Reinhart Koselleck contrasts the "horizon of expectation" with the "horizon of experience."[1] They are mutually connected by their contrariness. Political and personal expectations depend on what one has experienced, and what one has experienced is influenced by that which one had been expecting. Therefore, the horizon, that intrinsic threshold, changes: It is modified during the course of our experiences as that which lies on the other side and cannot be reached. In this sense, works of art and exhibitions also define a changing horizon that presents new perspectives in the form of ideas, of what can be imagined, and what cannot. Art offers proposals and produces images of what this world and other possible worlds might look like. Contemporary art thus establishes its own horizon, as Simon Sheikh argues: "An exhibition of art always sets up a horizon, a proposal of what can be imagined, and what cannot, and art therefore not only partakes in certain imaginaries, but it is also the producer of such imaginaries, and therefore potentially of other ways of imagining and imaging the world, as well as other possible worlds. Art has the capacity to thematize the very situating of the horizon, with its contingencies, histories, institutions, and struggles, as well as limits."[2]

The United Nations building in Prishtina is surrounded by a massive concrete wall. Since 1999, Kosovo has been involved in a nation-building process, which is supported to this day by the international community and the active involvement of NATO, UNO, UNMIK, and EULEX.

Concatenated concrete pylons form a tall, compact barrier which separates the UN building at the city limits from that very city. The concrete of the barriers was painted on the outside to downplay the appearance of a military safety zone. Different shades of blue were applied in broad wavy lines, apparently meant to represent an abstract landscape in an airy, Mediterranean way. The blue tones adhere to the principle of foreground, middle plane, background. The dark blue area on the wall's lower part is followed by a very light blue, which in turn is followed by turquoise, then a light gray-blue, and, finally, a type of light blue reminiscent of the sky on a slightly cloudy day. One would pay little mind to this painted wall, were it not for its stark contrast to a sandbag-covered watchtower located directly behind the wall, the defensive function of which is clear and unobscured by paintwork. Blue is the color of distance, of desire and yearning, of the sky. The flag of the European Union is also blue. This bright blue was not used to paint this wall, but it does resonate by way of association: Behind this insurmountable wall lies the other territory, the object of desire, the horizon that remains intangible. On the other hand, the UN building embodies not only the mandate of securing geographic borders, but also the infiltration of government administration. The employees of various international institutions and missions live in the country as emissaries, isolated from the populace. The reinforced concrete wall also visualizes this isolation, which replaces the principle of migration with that of being a transient guest.

Flaka Haliti has explored these striking concrete pylons that surround the UN building before, in other exhibitions. In one instance, she had a scale model built using MDF plates and painted it concrete gray. The paint camouflaged the lightness of the material. In an exhibition at Vienna's mumok the pylons were turned upside down, which made them seem like pillars and, therefore, part of the building's architecture. However, the adapted parts of the militarized protective wall also blocked the view of the images hung on the exhibition walls. They virtually obstructed the view of these photographs of abstract cloud formations. They also guided visitors through the gallery space as if through an obstacle course, thus rendering a complete long-shot view impossible. One had to step very close to the images to get a detailed view of them. The oppressive narrowness of the space was thus replaced by the view of openness and expanse.

I see a face. Do you see a face is the title of this photo series, in which Haliti transformed cloud formations into faces with a few computer-generated lines. The first sentence is a statement of fact; the second one is a question without a question mark. Thus the question-turned-statement indicates that the speaker need not have the statement confirmed by a second party. The speaker is sovereign in his or her perception of a circumstance. The children's game thus becomes a study about the subjective perspective of a natural constellation that can vary depending on the beholder. No consensus is necessary in order to see faces in clouds, because they are the products of an imagination that adheres to its own logic. One cannot verify it, but one can share or reject the interpretation, see another image altogether, or see condensed water vapor shaped like clouds.

Haliti's art makes its statements in a subtle way by incorporating the symbols of its surroundings and examining their political dimension from a subjective perspective. The horizon as a recurring motif in her works is no accident: as a political symbol and as a poetic image of a yearning for that which does not (yet) exist. For Haliti, art delineates a sphere of possibility that is within range of reality. She does not develop fictional scenarios in her works, but discusses the conditions of her everyday life: What does it mean to be an artist, to be from Kosovo, to not live there full-time, and also to only partly live elsewhere. Haliti lives in Munich, Vienna, and Prishtina—cities which are different but also bear similarities, and where the "wealth gap" as defined by sociologists is enormous. She regards all three places as part of her home, which, however, can never be one homogeneous home. This life is precarious, torn, and yet represents the reality of many. Flaka Haliti attempts to discuss loaded terminologies, such as those of migration and belonging, but without any grand gestures of political proclamation. By translating them into seemingly simple yet nonetheless complex metaphors, she imbues them with an intuitive presence, which we must find our relationship to. How we understand these works, therefore, always also depends on the relationship between our own horizon of expectations and our body of experience: Does the experience of migration and alienation from one's own country affect us? Do we know what it is like to exist between cultures? Do we possess the vocabulary necessary to consider the private as political? What do we wish for, what do we want or expect?

As a foreign exchange student at the Städelschule in Frankfurt am Main, Haliti examined the segregative community of expats in the German financial capital and conducted interviews with some of them. Audio tracks reminiscent of those from a language course attest to a relation to place, language, and the feeling of belonging that is fundamentally different from the migratory experience of others: "I came to Frankfurt for my job," "I don't speak German, as I don't need it for my daily occupations," "I feel international here." Haliti, on the other hand, was automatically taken for an immigrant because of her origin. However, her works are less about personal experiences than about the development of a language that can express and render communicable the emotions connected with them: love, loneliness, loss. These are categories that are generally deemed incapable of much discursive depth or political relevance and which, as a language of interiority, lead a marginal existence and are regarded more with cynical distance than with empathy when they are introduced into the fine arts. Haliti has therefore developed a sensitivity for designing spatial scenarios with simple means in which complex emotions can be physically transferred to the beholder and consequently speak intuitively of openness and expanse, confinement and trepidation.

One enters the almost square space of the Kosovo Pavilion through a narrow, high-walled entranceway. One can already see through this narrow opening that the walls inside are whiter than white. The bright, light color that seems to spread immaterially across the walls deprives them of their solidity and suggests a kind of transparency: The wall becomes a membrane behind which the space opens onto the exterior, onto the outdoors. It is an invisible horizon, a threshold. Blue sand covers the floor. Its colors are reminiscent of the paint on the hermetic protective wall in Prishtina, but without this reference the colors unfold their own connotations. Blue is a color with contrary connotations: The color of desire, of harmony, of romanticism, of the sky and the sea. The flag of Kosovo is blue like the flag of the European Union. It features five stars, which represent the country's ethnicities, and the outline of the country whose independence was recognized by only 109 of the 193 United Nations member states and whose political development is still supervised by EULEX Kosovo. The Western eye perceives blue as the most pleasant color of the spectrum. The European Union chose it to symbolize unity in diversity and the ability to find consensus. It is a color that conveys social codes and values, and has specific historical and geographic features. In the Western world alone, the color blue has experienced a social transformation and a plethora of interpretations throughout history. Non-existent in language and iconography until the end of the High Middle Ages, the color blue in liturgical imagery later became the color of the Virgin Mary and the signal of royalty par excellence. In the course of the centuries, the royal color became a political symbol of the Counter-Reformation and, later, of the French Revolution. Since then, blue has been integrated within a strictly codified value system and represents normalization: The color of infinity, of immateriality, and of the universe became the color of television screens. The color of the French Revolution became the color of conservatism and "liberal" parties. The color of workers became the color of the executive.

Everyone who enters the Kosovo Pavilion alters the blue texture of the floor and takes a few grains of sand with them. The space grows, expands. Like a molecule, it loses its shape when visitors distribute the sand and carry it beyond the pavilion's boundaries. Hence, there could be a lightness in this interplay of colors, the lucid horizon and the blue ground. But there are also large, towering sculptures within the space which echo the massive concrete pylons from Prishtina. Their massive presence robs the scenario of its lightness and obstructs the view of the yearnful expanse. They are abstract sculptures, although they quite obviously remind viewers of manifestations of power. At a towering height of almost ten feet, they dwarf the viewers. The structure of the reinforced concrete parts of the wall is visible in these sculptures and obscures their perception under formal-aesthetic aspects.

It is evident that they are a commentary on the situation in Kosovo, the experience of migration and homelessness, of the feeling of heteronomy, and the desire for the borders to disappear. And yet, the image of the obstructed view of the horizon may also be perceived on a more general level, where it describes a fundamental problem. Barriers present themselves as constructed manifestations of political decisions and territorial boundaries. They are exclusive and inclusive at once. But the horizon transcends the idea of the threshold, if we accept it as a suggestion of what to imagine. In this sense, one also enters this space in order to feel that one can leave behind one's spatial limitations.

The horizon is the absolute metaphor for the idea that one can only see and comprehend something if one focuses one's view and at the same time does not look at the threshold, but leaves it at the margin, at the periphery, in the background.[3] As a threshold of seeing and understanding that is neither visible nor invisible, the horizon renders seeing and understanding possible in the first place, and with them, delineation, differentiation, classification. It is the excluded third state of differentiation between visible and invisible: their unity and a condition for possibility. To the extent that it makes delineation possible and withdraws from it, the horizon is a background of classification. One sees a sculpture against the background of the wall, comprehends an event within the context and thus background of history—the metaphor of the background de-paradoxes the metaphor of the horizon.

One can approach the horizon, which will always be far away. One cannot cross it, but one can move it. It is therefore a spatial border, but not a temporal one. Each horizon bears new horizons. They are borders of delineation, but they are only temporary.

First published in *Flaka Haliti: Speculating on the Blue*, Venice Biennale, Sternberg Press, 2015.

1 Reinhart Koselleck, "'Space of Experience' and 'Horizon of Expectation': Two Historical Categories," in *Futures Past: On the Semantics of Historical Time* (Studies in Contemporary German Social Thought), trans. Keith Tribe, New York, Columbia University Press, 2004, pp. 255–275.

2 Simon Sheikh, "Vectors of the Possible: Art Between Spaces of Experience and Horizons of Expectations," in *On Horizons: A Critical Reader in Contemporary Art*, ed. Maria Hlavajova, Simon Sheikh, and Jill Winder, Rotterdam, BAK Utrecht, 2011, p. 160.

3 Cf. Werner Stegmeier, *Philosophie der Orientierung*, Berlin, de Gruyter, 2008, pp. 199–206.

I NEED A PILULE DU LENDEMAIN TO MAKE ME STOP FEELING BLUE

65 PERCENT UNDER 30
An interview with *Dardan Zhegrova* and *Astrit Ismaili*

Cathrin Mayer

In November 2018, I visited the city of Prishtina for the first time. Spending a couple of days there, I was struck by how much this new country, born out of the war, is driven by a new generation of millennials. Sixty-five percent out of Kosovo's population of two million is below the age of 30, and the birth rate is among the highest in Europe. This new generation has very limited mobility due to political issues, visa requirements, and Europe's discrimination towards Kosovo citizens. The core problem causing these circumstances is the refusal of other states[1] to recognize the legitimate sovereignty of Kosovo. This non-acceptance by other countries, interestingly enough, derives from inner political struggles these countries have with autonomous communities.[2] The question of acceptance is not directly linked to Kosovo *per se*, but to local, political issues and unrest within those countries that deny Kosovo's independence. From the perspective of those countries, Kosovo executed a worst case scenario when it created its state autonomously from Serbia. For this reason, not only the youth but the whole population is confronted with an impossible bureaucratic apparatus when applying for a visa to travel.[3] The young generation of Kosovars is caught between the future, which they naturally want to shape, and the past, which ten years after the declaration of independence,[4] is still not behind them. This specific vacuum makes it hard to trust in the belief system of today called globalization. On the contrary, it is a steady rejoinder to the promises of late capitalist dictums of interconnectivity and the assumption that geographical borders do not exist within Europe.

I interviewed Dardan Zhegrova (born 1991) and Astrit Ismaili (born 1991), both originally from Kosovo's capital Prishtina. The latter is not equipped with the conditions and infrastructures typical of art centers around the world, but even though the city is lacking a stable funding system for the arts and a reliable economy in general, it has a vibrant scene that—out of limitations and restrictions—makes it work along the line of experimentation. Therefore, artistic practices develop from the inside out rather than the other way around. While Dardan Zhegrova is an integral part of the vivid art scene in Prishtina, Astrit Ismaili received a student scholarship and moved to Amsterdam four years ago, where he is still based. Both of their practices are realized through a queer subjectivity and perspective. Since 2015, Astrit and Dardan have been represented by LambdaLambdaLambda, the only international commercial contemporary art gallery operating in the country.

I talked to both artists about their place within contemporary art production, queer subculture, and the future of the art scene in Kosovo.

CATHRIN MAYER *Reflecting on the mechanisms of contemporary art, one can say there is a certain fascination—predominantly in the West/Global North—with anything that seems not yet fully accessed. Of course this is an interest aligned with the general research of curators or gallerists into showcasing new discoveries. Do you think that because you are coming from the Former Socialist Federal Republic of Yugoslavia, a Balkan country, your art is contextualized differently?*

ASTRIT ISMAILI I have been dealing with contextualization and re-contextualization of my work specifically for four years, when I moved from Prishtina to Amsterdam for a performance master's program at DasArts. During this period, I felt pressure to label myself and my work so that my cultural background and the political situation in Kosovo would be an intrinsic part of my art practice. I was highly disturbed by this neoliberal way of categorizing and branding and therefore I have done my best to avoid victimization and not use it as a key to open doors in my career—which is what the West often expects of artists coming from postwar countries. To go beyond my personal story, I use speculative fabulation as a type of narration, with which I unfold realities and worlds I create, reaching universal issues.

I came up with *THE PREGNANT BOY* (2016), an alter ego, that arises from my personal history but develops further into fiction. *THE PREGNANT BOY* comes to earth from the Bubble Gum Satellite, falls in love with the sun, and becomes pregnant. *THE PREGNANT BOY* doesn't have a name, an ethnicity, a career, basically doesn't belong to any category and is always in contrast with every environment he is in. *THE PREGNANT BOY* is a symbol of resistance, standing for authenticity and the right to be undefined. I believe that labels strongly affect the process of growing and create boundaries that are hard to bend once they have already been invested in. Discovering *THE PREGNANT BOY* alter ego somehow freed me from the heavy weight of generalized representation formats that I felt uncomfortable carrying on my shoulders.

DARDAN ZHEGROVA Yes, I have sometimes noticed a different contextualization of our work because of our origin; us being connoted as "exotic." Most people have heard about Kosovo in the international news—mainly about the war and its trauma, and not much about the country's cultural roots has been communicated. However, this lack of knowledge about the art scene of Kosovo in the West drew the curiosity of curators to discover a scene that developed out of a postwar society, and which created its own aesthetic language.

C.M. *The word "subculture" has generally been used to describe various artistic movements within the course of the last century that were neglecting aligned artistic production and forms of living. In the West, its meaning was never fixed or fully determined, but shifted through time and politics. In the recent history of Eastern Europe, artistic production as a form of "subculture" meant sabotage and guerilla actions. Considering "subculture" today, it resides within ambivalent realities. It is partly dissolved within the logic of consumerism, existing as an empty phrase within marketing logic, offering a supposed experience of non-conformism. On the other hand, we are currently witnessing the increasing marginalization of certain groups in society on a global level. Immigrants and gays are more and more pushed into segregated forms of life. Considering those specific implications, do you consider queer life in Kosovo as a form of "subculture"?*

A.I. Growing up in Kosovo, there were no queer voices we could look up to. We had to start from scratch! With friends and other artists, we kind of organically created our little bubbles, in which we felt safe to express ourselves through our lifestyle and ideas on art. With Dardan, the girls of the HAVEIT group (Lola and Alketa Sylaj), the magazine KOSOVO 2.0, and the film festival DokuFest, among many other individuals and supporters, I believe we brought new aspects to the scene. I am happy to see that nowadays being queer in Kosovo feels much safer than ten years ago. Young trans activists like Lendi Mustafa and Blert Morina have spoken openly about their transitioning processes and this has bolstered many voiceless individuals. Last summer, I celebrated my 27th birthday in Prishtina. On that very day I attended a big queer party called *Prishtina Is Burning*, which was organized by Lendi Mustafa, Linda Suhodolli, and TADI, and took place at Klubi M and Termokiss (a community-run center in Prishtina). It was so touching to see so many people from the community and allies celebrating together openly. Everybody in Prishtina is saying that this is the most exciting subculture that is happening right now.

D.Z. Ideally, I wouldn't consider one's gender identity and sexual orientation as a subculture, in this case LGBTQ+, because it could be considered as a choice, something that one chooses to join or be part of. This means also that acceptance of it depends on someone's "taste" or ideas. I think gender identity and sexual orientation should be accepted by society at large regardless of cultural differences. On the other hand, "queer" as a subculture influences our lifestyle, how we dress, our looks, and the way we interact in society. As Astrit mentioned before, in Kosovo queerness started to become more visible in the late 2000s, and our group of friends has influenced the art scene by introducing “gender” to discussions in a way that challenges common ideas of what a man and a women and everything in between could be on the right, left, up, down, inside, outside.

The Pride Parade, happening since 2017 in Prishtina, raised awareness of the LGBTQ+ community among the general public, also by being showcased in national media across Kosovo. There is an urge to constantly talk about and raise this issue, so at some point it will become “normal.” Still, for a broad acceptance of LGBTQ+ we have a long way to go. Whom you love may cause a very hard life, with constant harassment and discriminiation here in Kosovo, but meanwhile kilometers away, like in Berlin, one can have quite an “ordinary” day without society mirroring the feeling you are behaving wrong. I think everyone who cares about other human beings should push this issue of equality of genders and the fight for equality of the LGBTQ+ community. With more presence in the media, people of influence coming out publicly, and organizations working hard to promote LGBTQ+ rights, all this could change the situation towards more common understanding and broader acceptance in society.

C.M. *I tried to research whether there is an Albanian or Serbian version of* Gender Trouble *by Judith Butler, which was published in its original version in 1991, but could not find any. How were you introduced to queer theory or the concept of queerness and are there any discussions or theories from a Kosovar perspective on this specific topic?*

D.Z. I don't think there is something specific on queer studies, except for a few papers on gender studies by the Kosovar Gender Studies Center. Some research was done on transgender people and homosexuality by organizations for LGBTI+ such as CEL (Center for Equality and Liberty) and CSGD (Center for Social Group Development). Personally, my own research on queerness was limited to the information I found online.

I consider myself queer, but not only because of my sexual orientation. Rather it's about being open to other gender identities and not classifying them as male or female. I cannot relate to the idea of what is expected in behaving/acting "male" in our society, in traditional and conservative terms. For our culture to grow, I feel a need to challenge societal norms of what is considered "ordinary."

A queer identity should be a new unifying identity for everyone as an open, non-judgmental way to present oneself. Being queer brings out the open-minded characteristics of a person, celebrating differences and influences from one another, with the will to experiment with the body, and with what we as human inherit, physically and psychologically.

My live poetry performance series *Lucky Pierre* (2016),[5] a fictional character I created, presents a fluid type of gender, which is not only defined by physical characteristics but rather by the poem it performs. *Lucky Pierre* translates emotions into words; it's a collection of love poems based on my personal experiences and feelings. The poems talk about one-sided love, sexual fantasies and daydreaming, oscillating between dream and reality. It can be understood as an embodiment of one's capacity to manipulate feelings, to reframe one's reality while time turns fluid, and as memories and dreams collapse in order to create your "own landscape." *Lucky Pierre* is an outlook to a fictional world of freedom for all genders.

A.I. There are a couple of NGOs that are passionately fighting for the rights of the LGBTQ+ community in Kosovo but there isn't yet a queer discourse. On the other hand, Kosovo's feminist movements and scholars have been the loudest on gender identity issues and in the past decades I can say that there has been a lot of progress on this matter. When it comes to queer theory, unfortunately, there isn't much available in the Albanian language. I personally got introduced to queer theory after I moved to the Netherlands, first by being part of the queer, non-binary, trans and POC communities. As a queer person, I think it is very important to appreciate and respect each other's specificities and experiences but at the same time, now more than ever, we must be in solidarity and stick together as a community against heteronormativity and the rise of fascism. In the times we are living in, our problems aren't local anymore, they surpass geographical borders. You can belong to a community even if you aren't physically present in it. This is empowering and therefore I find we should take advantage of it.

C.M. *Let's go back to the beginning of your artistic career. How is the art education in Prishtina, how did you experience it? And what, who influenced or formed your artistic practice?*

A.I. I finished my bachelor studies for theater directing in the class of Bekim Lumi in 2013. I was always interested in body politics, but I didn't want become a theater maker.

I always wanted to be a visual artist, but in Kosovo there wasn't a program for performance art at the Department of Visual Arts. Theater directing was the closest program to what I wanted to study. I was lucky to be mentored by Bekim Lumi, an icon of Kosovo's contemporary theater scene. He was one of the few professors who passionately tried to free the performance scene from its conservative approach. During those four years I learned how to find freedom within a very strict structure and not to depend so much on it. Parallel to my studies, I was pretty active in the visual arts scene, trying to build a bridge between theater and visual arts. An example is *Prishtine-mon amour,* a performance art event I co-curated at the burnt section of the Palace of Youth and Sports Boro & Ramizi in Prishtina in 2012. With major participation by local and international artists, we explored the notion of "repetition," creating a massive event that included disciplines as different as performance art, contemporary dance, ballet, theater, video, and installation. The significance of *Prishtine-mon amour* was our open approach to the community, aiming to interact with individuals and groups that function separately in different subcultures and disciplines.

D.Z. I always wanted to study film directing, but the Academy of Fine Arts was too conservative, with a curriculum from the communist period; therefore, I studied journalism for two years and worked as a journalist for KOSOVO 2.0 magazine.

The education system can restrict one from experimenting and developing a unique art practice. I was influenced neither by the Academy of Fine Arts, nor by artists of the academy. Rather I was influenced by my personal experiences and research I did with other artist friends of my generation. I had the freedom to experiment with how one can express ideas through different mediums, and how to develop my practice in writing.

So on the one hand, cinematography, photography, and fashion magazines influenced me; on the other, my childhood in my mother's workshop. She is a tailor and I was playing with and surrounded by textiles all my life. Since I was a child, I memorized the "touching" of fabrics, and had a sensibility for materials, and at some point in my practice I started to use fabric as a tool to form ideas for soft sculptures.

C.M. to D.Z. *You had a collective together with Astrit Ismaili called* The Evil Makers. *You were obsessed with watching movies and made your own ones. Was this the starting point for both of your artistic practices? And why was film so important back then?*

D.Z. I was always interested in art, music, and film. When I was twelve, I found a phone, with a low resolution pixel camera. I started using it and experimenting with it; made photos and short videos, recording my friends and imitating what I was seeing on TV or in fashion magazines. This opened a whole new world for me. So I could say, photography was the first "artistic medium" I experimented with.

In our teenage years, Astrit Ismaili, Lola and Alketa Sylaj (members of the HAVEIT group), Blerta Ismaili (an actress and Astrit Ismaili's sister), Gisha (Gresë Lahu), a makeup artist, and me, among others, were hanging out and sharing our passion for films. Somehow cinematography was a way for us to experience and feed ourselves with what was happening in the world, outside of Kosovo. We got inspired and relived moments from films like *The Dreamers* by Bernardo Bertolucci.

Together we did short experimental videos that imitated movie scenes, did photo sessions around the city, or we gathered and organized house parties, all dressed up. We used our fantasies to escape from our everyday lives and to create our own worlds.

We named our group *The Evil Makers* to try and change how society classifies good or bad, and we aimed to contrast “Beauty” from “Evil” to show another part of what was considered bad or evil.

In a way, those years were very important in shaping our identities and one can still see the influence of those years in our works (HAVEIT’s, Astrit’s, and mine).

Both your practices are very intertwined with the exploration of extended subjective realities. Whether it is through Dardan’s performative readings—which through the multiplication of the self allow for different characters and perspectives to appear—or through the performance THE NEW BODY *(2018) by Astrit in which the body extends to become a musical instrument.*

How do you think about subjectivity and the body in relation to your practice?

D.Z. In my practice and specifically in my performance work, my body becomes the subject and plays with the possibilities of transformation. Today, the reality of the human character is so intertwined with the surrealism of the virtual world, so my performances show a different way of layering your personality and how one deals with one’s self through what one chooses to use as a representation. Our memories are the base on which we are built and we have the possibility to decide on what and how to remember. Daydreaming can be a tool for manipulating our reality to merge with our imagination. Personally, this is a necessity when it comes building our identity and creating our own narrative.

In a way, we are whoever we want to be and "being" is a temporary fluid state, influenced by our communication with the "world."

A.I. I am fascinated by the process of becoming and the possible shapes and states a body can achieve, and further in the body's political voice and its strength to question social constructs and codes of behavior. The body in my practice is a medium in which I examine and express different emotions and ideas, mostly through transforming, making of sounds, singing and poetry.

You mentioned *THE NEW BODY*, an outcome of my long research on future bodies and gene editing technologies, which I guess will soon revolutionize the way we view the human body in relation to technology and identity politics.

For the performance *THE NEW BODY*, I designed a wearable musical instrument that can be activated with physical movements, which trigger sounds of voices I have recorded. The structure of the instrument transforms the silhouette of the human body and adds new physical attributes to it. During the performance, I execute a music composition that I wrote for the instrument while I am simultaneously singing. The shift from live to avatar performance can thus be considered a way of relating to human bodies outside the temporal and spatial confines of performance. The experience of being in this “new body” is similar to being in a cage. Physically, it is challenging to keep the instrument silent, and its structure adds new qualities in the movement of the body by limiting its range of functions. The only way to find freedom in such a body is to get into a state of trance, by repetitive movement and singing. Thus, I discovered an interesting meeting point between spirituality and technology. By translating the body’s gestures into sound, I aim at disrupting prevailing narratives around representation, imagining new and utopian ways of thinking about how bodies inhabit and occupy space. *THE NEW BODY* is a clash of subjectivity and objectivity; its sound is a representation of this conflict and the struggle to find harmony in limitation.

C.M. to A.I. *The aesthetics and the vocabulary of your performances seem to come from an examination of contemporary popular culture. In* EMO GIRL *(2018), for example, you are running in circles together with seven other performers, among them your sister. Each character is ascribed a different color and is highly stylized, outfitted including makeup. You start to sing in the beginning only “Oh I” repeatedly and then your fellow performers tune in, in the same rhythm with phrases like “Never work” or “Oh Why?”. The rhythmic pace collapses at some point when the bodies dramatically fall on the floor, tearing each other down and lingering there. In the next moment, you see them leaning against the wall asserting themselves in fashion poses, resembling a Benetton campaign from the ’90s. I remember the moment of change and collapse from the choreography* EMO GIRL *as very vivid; it revealed emotional instability and how one's own body is always relative to the bodies surrounding you. Could you describe how affirmation and subversion function for you as a tool and where your fascination for pop culture comes from? Does pop culture in Kosovo have some unique characteristics and phenomena?*

A.I. *EMO GIRL* is a new cult-like community inspired by the Emo-Goth/Rock subcultures that were very present in Kosovo in the early 2000s. The emo music movements are generally associated with youth who are dispirited and angry at society, people, or themselves. Performing pain or dark emotions often creates a distance, which can help one to regenerate and heal. *EMO GIRL* is a coping mechanism for complex emotions presented through melodies, lyrics, and choreographies, performed by femme, queer, and non-binary bodies. In contrast to the 2000s emo music subcultures, *EMO GIRL* proposes an unconventional aesthetic of "darkness" that is still quite sad and heavy but is catchy, like pop music, and colorful and seductive like candy. There is a phrase we are all singing during *EMO GIRL*: "...if you don't want to work now, how are you going to be a star..." This phrase summarizes best the paradox of how *EMO GIRL* deals with its critical views of a system that violently reduces our bodies to labor, but also the obsession with stardom, which is seen as a path to self-fulfillment and validation.

My fascination with pop music started very early. When I was a teenager, I worked for the radio. My job was to explore new music so I had to listen to pop, even though in this period I was more into trip hop or even death/black metal music. This is how my curiosity for discovering new singers, producers, record labels and the whole pop music industry got started, but more for research than entertainment. Also, having had a singing career as a duo with my sister for six years in Kosovo as a child pop star has strongly affected my artistic practice. The process of becoming a pop star made me think about the politics invested in the construction of identities and public personas. It made me conscious of the power inherent in the voice and its cultural impact on society. Pop music influences millions of people by often being an instrument of change. On the other hand, pop music as an industry can also reinforce problematic issues. When it simply mirrors normative sides of reality without responsibility or constructive criticism, it just becomes another tool of structural oppression.

Kosovo has a super rich pop music scene. Although it is quite generic, there are so many pop stars and only a few are pretty good and doing well internationally. Considering the small population of Kosovo, it produces way more pop music than most of the other European countries.

C.M. to D.Z. *You seem to be very interested in speech and its visual representation. The basis for your works is text and poetry, which seem to stem from you own lived experiences, but also from a space of imagination. You mostly write from a first-person perspective, addressing a desired subject. In your continuous series called* Your enthusiasm to tell a story *(ongoing since 2015) you create larger-than-life characters, which carry a sound device that plays a designated piece of poetry for each "voodoo doll." The logic of the works does not seem to allow a detachment from the self and the other, or the subject of desire and the desired one. This psychological moment is a central motive in your artistic production, in which the constitution of the self transpires through fiction. Do you think the fictional becomes a tool in your work and for yourself that enables you to travel, if not physically, mentally? And how important is, for example, the virtual world (internet) to you?*

D.Z. The open series *Your enthusiasm to tell a story* is an ongoing project, which I started with *Your enthusiasm to tell a story (Yellow)* for an exhibition I was part of at LambdaLambdaLambda in 2015. So far, the series consist of seven larger-than-life voodoo dolls. It started with the need to translate a very personal intimate poem into a physical sculpture as a substitute for physical interaction with the subject of the poem.

I do this by writing poems that depict my projections onto a relationship, and then record them with my own voice. This spoken poem (on a mp3-player) is placed into the voodoo doll where the heart is located. The color of the respective dolls is derived from the color of the poem that in turn is always based on a certain emotion I associated with that color.

The objects are based on voodoo dolls since one tries to access another person remotely through activating those dolls in one way or another.

I wanted to use the idea of magic and how people, when feeling a lack of something, want to replace it with a "token" to represent that certain need. So each doll is a "token" for symbolizing what I really missed in all of those relationships. In this aspect, the poetry gave me the freedom to experience something that was not happening, and the dolls gave me a chance to literally build this imagination based on real encounters. In a sense, sometimes something that doesn't happen leaves room for more; its a seed of a new world—so these dolls live a fictional life by telling a factual story.

In the case of the "dolls," however, the idea is being reversed—one needs to get in close proximity in order to hear a poem/story that is very personal. I explore the physical as well as emotional proximity and distance, and hence all the emotional tropes that are distributed along this axis.

The internet has changed the way we communicate, the way we think and the way we perceive, and how we receive all kinds of (channeled) information. I find it inspiring that what is considered real or a reality has started to shift and change. Everything we see online is in a way edited or retouched. The communication between people no longer has to be physical, ideas are spread way faster, and it's possible to have multiple parallel identities or virtual lives. All this had an influence on the visual aesthetics of my work.

Further, living in a country with limited freedom to travel, the internet has become a tool to connect to the world "outside," to be connected to the Western world. So somehow we live in a physical world of Kosovo and the virtual world of the world.

C.M. *If we look to the future, how do you imagine the Kosovo art scene five years from now?*

D.Z. I expect more unconventional ideas, more experimentation, more underground culture, and I am sure there is potential for young queer artists and performers to challenge conservative ideas, religion, sexism, homophobia, and I would say: kill your darlings, kill your idols, kill your "parents" #wink.

A.I.
Let's dream…

In five years, Kosovo's independence will be fully recognized.
Its citizens will travel without visas.
Its artists will finally feel like they belong to a larger network than their geographical localities.
International artists will move to Kosovo because it's cheap, vibrant and unique, and this will make the scene culturally diverse.
The art schools will shut down and be replaced with open labs, frequent workshops, temporary programs led by local and international key figures of contemporary art.
More independent art spaces.
More queer spaces.
More squats.
More music festivals.
A richer performance scene.
And on and on and on…

1 European countries that do not recognize Kosovo as a state are Spain, Greece, Cyprus, Romania, Slovakia, and Serbia.

2 Such as, for example, Spain and Catalonia.

3 Visa-free travel is only possible to Albania, Dominica, Ecuador, Gambia, Haiti, Macedonia, Micronesia, Montenegro, Panama, Turkey, and Serbia, among others.

4 Kosovo declared independence in 2008.

5 *Lucky Pierre* refers in slang to the male in the middle of a threesome (sex act of three people), who is the active and the passive at the same time.

WILD BEAST

About the Authors

Sezgin Boynik (born 1977 in Kosovo) is a theoretician and publisher based in Helsinki, Finland. He has completed a PhD on the political aspect of Yugoslav "Black Wave" cinema. He has published on structuralist films, cultural nationalism, hard-core punk, and conceptual art, and is editor of *Rab-Rab: journal for political and formal inquiries in art.*

Charles Esche (born 1962 in England) is director of the Van Abbemuseum, Eindhoven, the Netherlands.

Alush Gashi (born 1975 in Serbia) is a cultural media specialist and director of Kino ARMATA, a public space promoting alternative culture and social dialogue in Prishtina, Kosovo.

HAVEIT (Hana Qena, born 1988 in Kosovo; Vesa Qena, born 1991 in Kosovo; Arbërore Sylaj, born 1988 in Kosovo; and Alketa Sylaj, born 1991 in Kosovo) is an art collective established in 2011 and based in Prishtina, Kosovo.

Astrit Ismaili (born 1991 in Kosovo) is a performance artist.

Shkëlzen Maliqi (born 1947 in Kosovo) is a philosopher, art critic, and political analyst.

Cathrin Mayr (born 1991 in Austria) is assistant curator at KW Institute for Contemporary Art, Berlin, Germany.

Miran Mohar (born 1958 in Slovenia) is a visual artist and member of the collective Irwin, based in Ljubljana, Slovenia.

Edi Muka (born 1969 in Albania) is an art critic and curator based in Stockholm, Sweden.

Vanessa Joan Müller (born 1968 in Germany) is Head of Dramaturgy at Kunsthalle Wien, Austria.

Kathrin Rhomberg (born 1963 in Austria) is artistic director of the Kontakt Art Collection, Austria.

Vesa Sahatçiu (born 1981 in Kosovo) is a writer and art historian. She studied art history and contemporary art theory at Goldsmiths, London, and the University of Auckland, New Zealand.

Dardan Zhegrova (born 1991 in Kosovo) is a visual artist and poet.

Notes on Contemporary Art in Kosovo

Editor
Katharina Schendl

Co-editors
Bardhi Haliti and Dren Maliqi

Texts
Sezgin Boynik
Charles Esche
Alush Gashi
HAVEIT
Astrit Ismaili
Shkëlzen Maliqi
Cathrin Mayr
Miran Mohar
Edi Muka
Vanessa Joan Müller
Kathrin Rhomberg
Vesa Sahatçiu
Dardan Zhegrova

Translations
Rozafa Maliqi (interview Shkëlzen Maliqi and Edi Muka)
Tamara Soban (essay Miran Mohar)

Proofreading
Rosemary Heather
Jennifer Taylor

Graphic design
Bardhi Haliti

Photo credit
Atdhe Mulla

Printed by Medienfabrik, Graz

A tranzit.at book

Published by
Sternberg Press
Caroline Schneider
Karl-Marx-Allee 78
D-10243 Berlin
www.sternberg-press.com

ISBN 978-3-95679-462-9

This publication has been made possible by the generous support of ADA, Austrian Development Cooperation;
ERSTE Foundation;
Ministry of Culture, Youth and Sports of the Republic of Kosovo;
Municipality of Prishtina;
tranzit.at *at.tranzit.org*

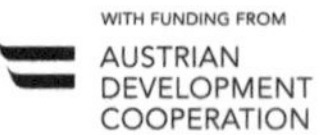

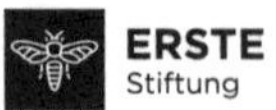

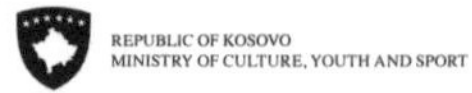

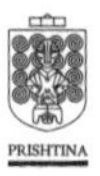

tranzit.at

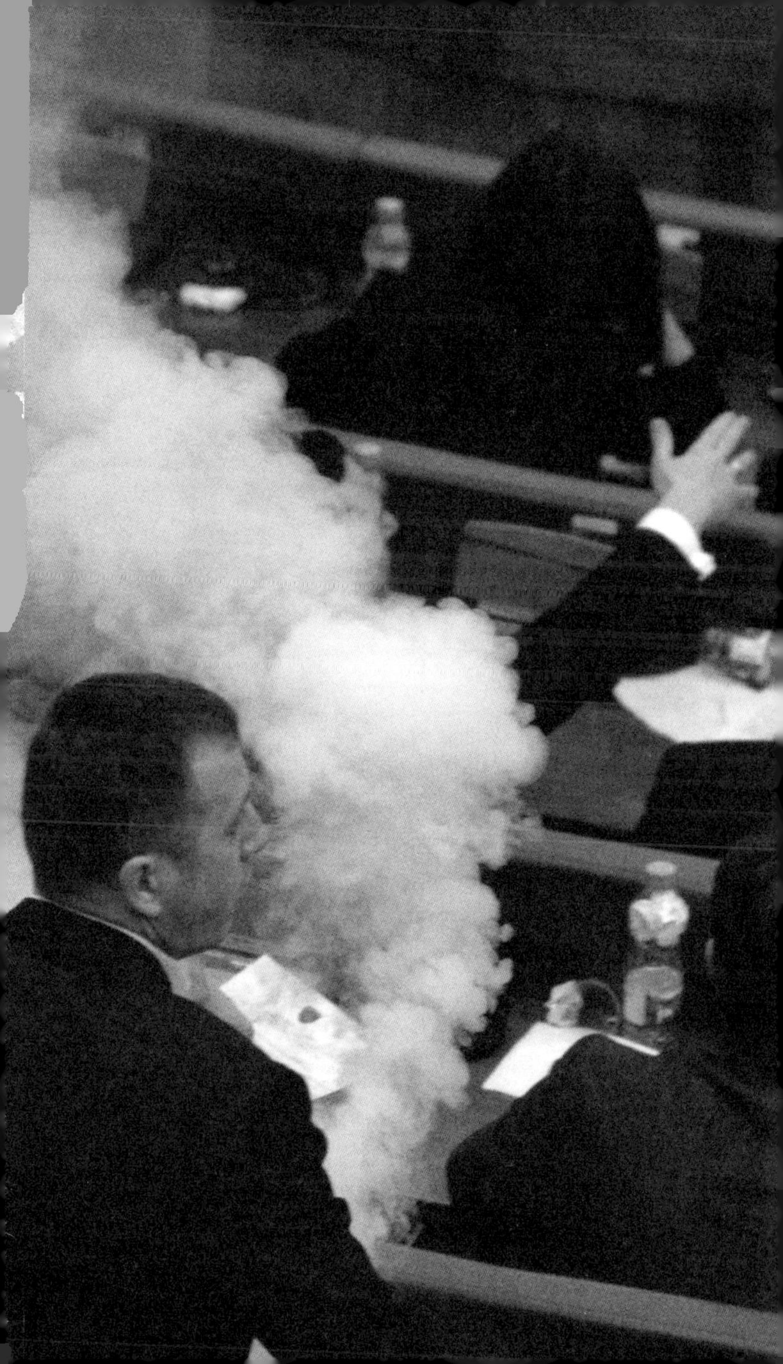

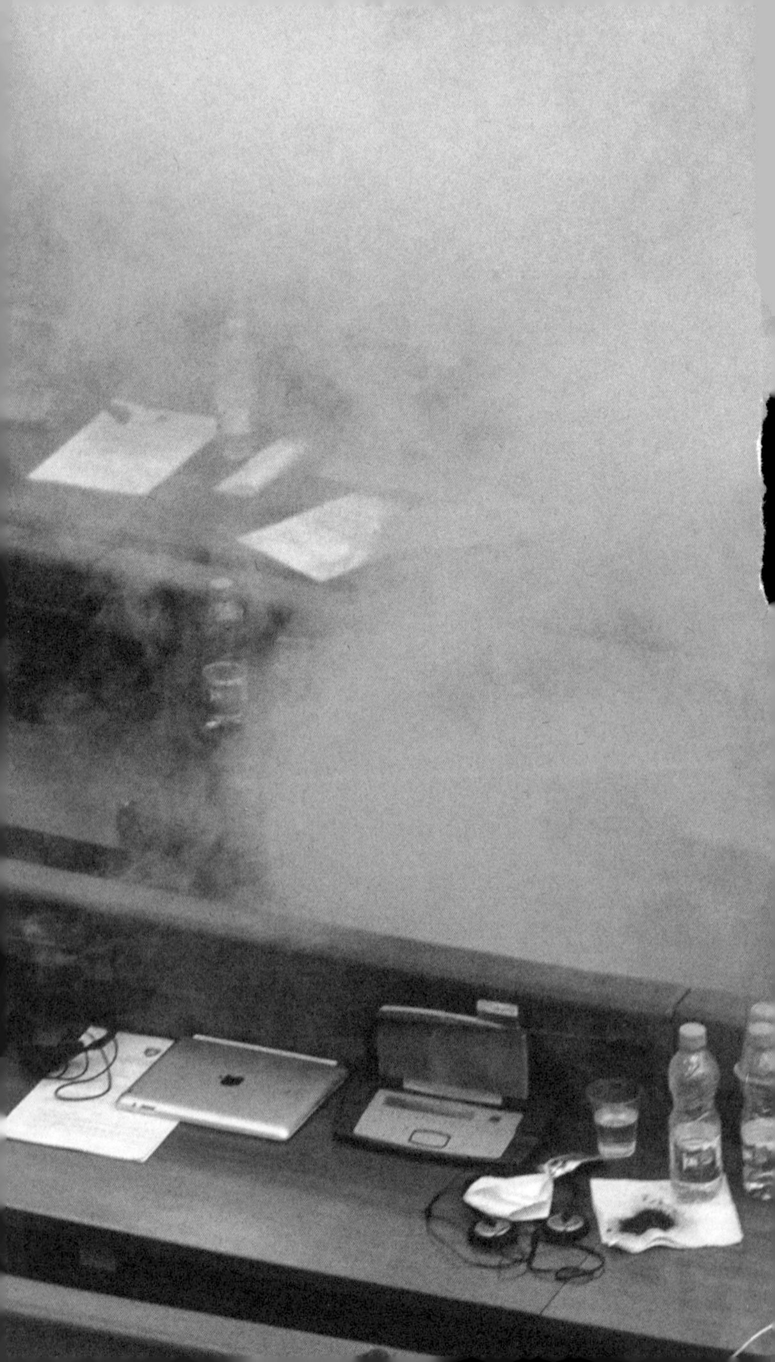